ANGELO POLIZIANO
* * *
SILVAE

EDITED AND TRANSLATED BY

CHARLES FANTAZZI

THE I TATTI RENAISSANCE LIBRARY
HARVARD UNIVERSITY PRESS
CAMBRIDGE, MASSACHUSETTS
LONDON, ENGLAND
2004

Series design by Dean Bornstein

Library of Congress Cataloging-in-Publication Data

Poliziano, Angelo, 1454–1494.
[Sylvae. English & Latin]
Silvae / Angelo Poliziano ; edited and translated by Charles Fantazzi.
p. cm. — (The I Tatti Renaissance Llibrary ; 14)
Includes bibliographical references and index.
Text in English and Latin.
ISBN 0-674-01480-4 (alk. paper)
1. Didactic poetry, Latin (Medieval and modern) — Translation into English.
2. Classical literature — History and criticism — Poetry.
3. Mythology, Classical — Poetry.
I. Fantazzi, Charles.   II. Title.   III. Series.
PA8563.S9513 2004
871'.04 — dc22   2004040516

Contents

ॐ࿐ॐ

Introduction

꿍Ꭽ꿍

In the colophon of his *Miscellanea,* a collection of short philological essays, the great Florentine scholar-poet Angelo Poliziano (1454– 1494) paid proud homage to two of his teachers: Marsilio Ficino, praised as a new Orpheus who had brought back from the dead the true Eurydice, i.e., the wisdom of Plato; and the Byzantine émigré John Argyropoulos, who had taught him Aristotelian philosophy. Poliziano admits, however, that he followed the lessons of the latter with sleep-filled eyes since he was more naturally attracted by the blandishments of the poet Homer.[1] Poetry was Poliziano's art, not philosophy. One of the finest Neo-Latin poets of the Renaissance, his poetry had from his earliest youth been inseparable from his scholarship. Indeed, at the tender age of fifteen, Angelo Ambrogini—called Poliziano or (in Latin) Politianus, from the name of his birthplace, Montepulciano—presented to Lorenzo de' Medici a translation of the second book of the *Iliad* in elegant Virgilian hexameters. In the next few years he completed the translation of Books 3–5. His proficiency in Greek was strengthened by his studies with Andronicus Callistus, a Byzantine émigré who arrived in Florence in 1471 to succeed Argyropoulos at the Florentine *Studio* or university. It was probably Callistus who introduced Poliziano to Hellenistic poetry, for it was at this time that he copied out more than four hundred epigrams from the *Greek Anthology,* an experience that inspired him to write his own Greek epigrams in various meters and dialects.

In 1473, at the age of nineteen, he was invited to live in the Medici palazzo in Via Larga as Lorenzo's private secretary and as tutor to his son, Piero. With free access to the extraordinary resources of Lorenzo's library, he sedulously pursued his philological studies and produced an impressive body of poetry in Greek,

Latin and Tuscan. In 1478, when a plague broke out in Florence, he was obliged to spend several dismal, rainy months in the Medici villa of Cafaggiolo in the Mugello with Lorenzo's wife, Clarice Orsini, a woman of little culture, and the two sons of Lorenzo, Piero and Giovanni. Sharp differences arose between Madonna Clarice and Poliziano concerning the education of Giovanni, who was destined for an ecclesiastical career, leading to the tutor's dismissal by Clarice the following spring. In the meantime Lorenzo had set off for Naples on a perilous diplomatic mission to King Ferrante of Aragon in order to negotiate a peace treaty to end the war that followed the Pazzi conspiracy.

Poliziano took offense at not having been invited to accompany him and suddenly left Florence for the North of Italy, where he became acquainted with the leading lights of Venetian humanism, Ermolao Barbaro, Girolamo Donà and Giorgio Merula, among others. In the spring of 1480, however, he wrote a long apologetic letter to Lorenzo and was received back into the good graces of his friend and patron. He was recalled to Florence and was appointed to the chair of poetry and rhetoric (*ars poetica et oratoria*) at the University of Florence. His inaugural lecture (or *praelectio*) in the fall of 1480 was an *Oration on Quintilian and Statius' Sylvae*, the opening words of which are designed to preempt expected criticism and at the same time to introduce his new program of literary studies. He acknowledges that critics will question his entering upon new and untrodden paths, and that even friends and fair-minded persons will wonder why he chose these second-rate authors, neglecting the princes of eloquence, Virgil and Cicero. The new professor is here indirectly alluding to his famous teacher and predecessor, Cristoforo Landino, who had lectured on these very authors in previous years. The reason for his choice is simple, he explains: it is easier for students to imitate authors who are more accessible to them rather than to strive immediately to scale the heights, just as a farmer provides props and stakes for the young vine to support its early growth. In reality, this new curriculum was an audacious departure from traditional teaching methods as practiced in Florence, and by introducing such authors as Statius (who had recently been edited by the Roman professor Domizio Calderini), and Quintilian (who had been the subject of Lorenzo Valla's controversial essay, *A Comparison of Cicero and Quintilian*), Poliziano seemed to be directly competing with the Roman school of philology.

Poliziano argues that there is no lack of richness of invention, grandeur of diction, rhetorical ornamentation, sententious sayings and magnificent metaphors in Statius, and he dares to say that Quintilian's *Institutiones oratoriae*, which undertakes to describe the formation of the orator from the cradle to full maturity, is fuller and richer than Cicero's rhetorical works. It is not that he wishes to detract from the sacrosanct glory of Cicero but rather to help the students approach the eloquence of Cicero through the mediation of Quintilian. He maintains that, although some ancient authors had the misfortune, through no fault of their own, of being discarded and lost in the age of the barbarians and have come down to us mutilated and truncated, we should not perpetuate their neglect and obscurity but welcome them back to the Latinity which they helped to create. The accusation that those authors lived at a time when eloquence was corrupt is false, for on closer inspection, he asserts, we shall see that it was not a question of decadence, but simply that the style of speaking (*genus dicendi*) had changed. To support his argument Poliziano quotes a controversial phrase from Tacitus: *Neque autem statim deterius dixerimus quod diversum sit* ("We should not say that what is different is automatically worse").[2]

The literary and pedagogical principles outlined in this speech are of great importance for understanding the style and the substance of the *Silvae*, Poliziano's poetic prolusions to his university lectures in subsequent years. The *Silvae*, indeed, not only contain some of the finest Latin poetry of the Renaissance, but afford unique insight into the poetical credo of a brilliant scholar. In Poliziano's innovative view of literary history each poet must be evaluated according to his genre and poetic practice. Poets from every period of classical antiquity and even modern times had something to offer the aspiring poet. Imitation should never be servile but should be an instrument to find one's own unique poetic voice. In his own tribute to Virgil, the *Manto*, he does not disdain to use phrases from minor poets together with those of Virgil to create his own new amalgam. His criterion in the choice of authors to imitate was elegant diversity, not canonicity. This was a criterion that reflected his own readings, his long years of studying and interpreting classical texts. A finished, individual style demanded scholarship and learning. In Poliziano there was no sudden metamorphosis from philologist to poet, or vice versa, nor was there any artificial dichotomy between the two. He is the quintessential scholar-poet, whether tossing off the more carefree vernacular verse of his youth as a member of Lorenzo's *brigata*, or polishing the learned Alexandrian poetry of the *Silvae*, in which the pedagogical intent becomes more prominent.

In the case of Poliziano it is possible for us to peer behind the scenes and observe the poet at work in the patient labor of transcribing, collating, emending, editing, commenting and interpreting the classical texts. For we are in possession of numerous manuscripts and incunabula annotated in his own hand—such as his copy, with copious notes, of the 1471 *Vergilius Romanus* published by Sweynheym and Pannartz—as well as notebooks, diaries and even student notes from his university lectures. A whole series of commentaries based on his lectures on Statius, Terence, Persius, Ovid, Suetonius and others has been published by the students of that incomparable master of humanistic philology, Alessandro Perosa. These annotations and commentaries of the poet constitute the raw material that will then be transformed, as if by a magic alembic, into the ornate and learned verse of the *Silvae*.

The choice of Statius' *Sylvae*[3] as the poetic work to be elucidated in his first university lecture is significant since it anticipates the title and style that Poliziano will use for his own poetic prolusions. In the introductory paragraphs to his commentary on Statius' poems, he elaborates on the meaning of the word *silva*, which he says denotes *indigesta materia*, a sort of confused raw material that the poet has to re-work. It has the connotation of looseness of structure, a sense of spontaneity and discontinuity. Statius himself had emphasized these qualities in his prefatory letter to the *Sylvae*, using expressions that suggested rapidity of composition and improvisation. But it is a studied, controlled improvisation that is achieved by long labor. The flexible style of the *silva* allows for both epic grandeur and bucolic simplicity, varied stylistic artifice, multiplicity of themes, all seasoned with rare literary erudition. The *Silvae* have a double nature. They are at one and the same time exquisitely learned poetry and a university lecture. Presented in an elegant and persuasive rhetorical framework, they illustrate the *docta varietas* which was Poliziano's poetic creed.

In the late spring of the same academic year, 1480–81, in which he lectured on Quintilian and Statius, Poliziano commented on the recently discovered "Epistle of Sappho to Phaon", considered to be one of Ovid's *Heroides*, a topic which must have been a pleasant diversion for his students after the grave theorizing of the first course. In his notes for these lectures his innovative approach is again plainly evident. Rather than a mere grammatical commentary, they provide a minute rhetorical analysis of the poem as an example of the genre *conquestio*, or lament. Poliziano is also interested in reconstructing Sappho's life and literary personality, aspects of which he will later include in the *Nutricia*. Noticeable also, in contrast to traditional commentaries, are the frequent quotations from ancient Greek literature, both in the original and in translation, as well as citations from Byzantine scholia and commentaries.

In the following year he turned to the *Rhetorica ad Herennium* and Ovid's *Fasti*, a text that had attracted much attention among Renaissance scholars, especially at the *Accademia Romana*, which fostered the study of Roman antiquities. One of their members, Paolo Marsi, was lecturing on the Ovidian poems in that very year and would publish his commentary in Venice in the summer of 1482. His was the usual didactic exercise, while the notes of Poliziano are more diffuse and contain many digressions, in the manner of his commentary on Statius. What interests Poliziano in the *Fasti* are the descriptions of liturgical rites and the origins of myth, etymology, geography and historical anecdote.

Of the four *praelectiones* that make up the *Silvae*, the first three (*Manto, Rusticus, Ambra*) were published a few days after their delivery: *Manto* on 9 November 1482, *Rusticus* on 26 October 1483, and *Ambra* shortly after 4 November 1485 (the date of the dedicatory letter to Lorenzo Tornabuoni). These were the only Latin or Greek poems Poliziano authorized for publication during his lifetime, save for a single ode in Landino's edition of Horace and the translation of two Greek epigrams in the *Miscellanea*. The *Manto* and *Rusticus* issued from the Florentine publishing house of Antonio Miscomini and the *Ambra* from that of Niccolò di Lorenzo, and no doubt were subjected to the scrutiny of the author. The editorial history of the *Nutricia* is more complex. According to a subscription in a later reprinting by Platone de' Benedetti (Bologna, 1491), the work was completed in Fiesole on the 8 October 1486. It had previously been entitled *Nutrix* and was destined for King Matthias Corvinus of Hungary, perhaps in the hope of gaining an entrée to the court of the king; but nothing came of this enterprise. He obviously took pride in the technical perfection, the brilliant *inventio* and the prodigious learning of these compositions. It was altogether a virtuoso performance.

The *Manto*, named after the prophetess, daughter of Tiresias, who gave her name to the city of Mantua, Virgil's birthplace, is preceded by a preface in elegiac distichs, a convention that goes back to the panegyric verse of the Silver Age of Latin literature. The scene is set in the cave of the centaur Chiron, as the Argonauts are about to set out on their voyage. Orpheus, one of the participants in that mythic journey, takes up his lyre and all of nature falls victim to his spell. When he lays down his instrument the young Achilles eagerly takes it up and produces a crude song which draws laughter from the guests. But Orpheus is pleased with his attempts, as Poliziano hopes Virgil will be glad to accept his own poetic homage.

The usual form of the *praelectio* consisted first of a *laudatio* of the writer to be studied and of his works, followed by a *cohortatio* to the students to encourage them in their emulation of the author. Most of the poem is a sustained encomium of Virgil and a subtle literary analysis of his works, consisting first of a rehearsal of the themes of poems once attributed to Virgil, the so-called *Appendix Vergiliana*, which was transmitted in all the early printed editions of Virgil, and then proceeding to the *Bucolics*, *Georgics* and *Aeneid*. In describing the individual works, the poet artfully inserts single words and phrases from the works themselves, constructing a rich mosaic of Virgilian diction interspersed with other poetic styles and patterns. But before introducing this customary thematic material, the poet depicts the dread goddess, Nemesis, taking many details from a description of Phidias' statue of her found in Pausanias' *Description of Greece*. It is a strange passage, mysteriously beautiful in itself, a caution about the temptation to hybris even in artistic creation, recalling his words in the dedicatory letter concerning the ephemeral quality of his offering. Poliziano seems to have two funeral laments of Statius in mind, *Sylvae* 2.4 and 2.6 on the death of two young boys. This grim figure appears also in the beautiful epicedion Poliziano wrote on the death of the fifteen-year old Albiera degli Albizzi. He seems almost to have had a morbid fascination with the role of Nemesis, often an unjust goddess, in the affairs of men. The exhortation to the young students at the end is an exuberant acclamation of eloquence and the sacred calling of the poet.

The *Rusticus* is an introduction to the reading of Hesiod's *Works and Days* and Virgil's *Georgics*. It is perhaps the most congenial and accessible of the *Silvae* with its lovely vignettes of country life made up both of descriptions of ancient farming in Virgil and Hesiod and of the contemporary Florentine countryside. To the usual ancient sources Poliziano adds the more technical treatises of Cato, Varro and Columella. In the case of the first two we are in possession of the collation made by Poliziano himself in 1482 of the *editio princeps* of *Scriptores rei rusticae* (Venice, 1472) from a codex in the library of San Marco in Florence.

Poliziano effects an easy transition from the bucolic to the georgic by having the shepherd Tityrus, a symbolic figure of Virgil, approach the poet on the banks of the Mincio and hand him the rustic pipe, bidding him to renew the Ascrean song, i.e., the poem of Hesiod. Next follows a eulogy of country life, incorporating the commonplaces of this theme, the moral rectitude of the countryman and the profusion of simple blessings. Entering into the heart of the poem, Poliziano describes the tasks of the various seasons, the building of the plough, the sowing of crops, but he softens the grim realism of Hesiod with delightful details, culminating in the marvelous *ekphrasis* of the perfect horse. He dwells on the pleasant pastimes of the countryman at every time of the year, the rustic feasts, the *vendemmia*, with the new wine flowing, and decorates this portion of the poem with colorful asides like the mock-heroic depiction of the arrogant cock, undisputed monarch of the courtyard. Verses 172–282 are an inspired hymn to spring, modeled on Lucretius' prologue to Venus in the *De rerum natura* and Virgil's similar passage in the second book of the *Georgics*, with some reminiscences also of Claudian's *Rape of Proserpine* as well as the garden of earthly delights, the realm of Venus, in his own vernacular composition, the *Stanze per la giostra* (1.77 ff.). The last part of the poem is devoted to the lunar calendar and to meteorological lore drawn from the last part of Aratus' poem, the *Phaenomena*, to which he adds interesting prognostic observations from the behavior of birds, the latter material derived from the eighteenth book of Pliny's *Natural History*. All of these borrowings he blends into verse of luminous lyricism and harmony. In the *envoi* to his poem—in imitation of Virgil, who ends the *Georgics* with an encomiastic farewell to the Emperor Augustus—Poliziano salutes Lorenzo, who provided him the leisure to write the poem at the Medici villa in Fiesole.

Ambra was the old name of another Medici villa at Poggio a Caiano (as it is now called). Lorenzo himself had celebrated the location in a narrative poem of his own, familiarly known as *Ambra*, a name given to it by the English historian, William Roscoe, in his famous biography of Lorenzo published in 1796. In the conclusion of the poem Poliziano, re-echoing Lorenzo but modifying his form of the myth, personifies the villa as a nymph, daughter of the Ombrone, tributary of the Arno, thus lending an aura of divinity to the villa as Statius had done in several of his *Sylvae* which are descriptions of villas.

The subject of this third prolusion is the exaltation of the poetry of Homer, font of all poetry and eloquence, "from whose gushing torrent all poets imbibe their secret frenzies." Like a magnet he draws all after him in the mighty chain of being. Much of the content of the poem is a versification of material that he delivered in a prose version, the *Oratio in expositione Homeri*. In both lectures Poliziano drew his material from the lives of Homer by the pseudo-Herodotus and pseudo-Plutarchus, available to him in Lorenzo's library. To herald the divine birth of Homer he constructs a compelling neo-pagan mythological framework, rich in recondite sources, including Homer himself and Statius, while for the eloquent lament of Thetis (vv. 92–112) he draws on the *Posthomerica* of Quintus Smyrnaeus, an epic poet of the third century AD. The display of learning in all of this is quite astounding. As he had summarized the Virgilian poems in the *Manto*, so here Poliziano gives a rapid compendium of the plots of the *Iliad* and the *Odyssey*. For the latter he employs a clever narrative device, having Ulysses appear to Homer and exhort him not to neglect his exploits, but to immortalize them in another great poem. The last part of the prolusion is taken up with an extended eulogy of the poet and the proclamation of the universal character of Homeric poetry: "And as Ocean, the parent of the elements, supplies the springs and rivers of the great earth, so from these pages every grace flowed down through the learned mouths of men." In a concluding homage to the poet Poliziano dedicates to him the garland of poetry woven from the flowers of the Muses that the nymph Ambra had given him.

The last and longest of the *Silvae* does not celebrate any single poet but rather poets and poetry itself from earliest mythical times to Poliziano's own day. As the title of his poem the poet uses a technical term from Roman law, *nutricia*, the remuneration paid to the nurse who nurtured a child. His own nurse was a goddess, the sister of the Muses, *Poetica*, who carries off human minds to the secret recesses of the starry heavens. He feels himself moved by some irresistible impulse, to which he willingly yields. Poliziano was conscious that he had entered upon a higher theme, and he mentions in the dedicatory letter to Antoniotto Gentili, an influential prelate at Rome, that it was the result of much recondite reading and much labor. In the previous dedication of the poem to King Matthias Corvinus of Hungary, he had given even more emphasis to the learned aspect and had promised a commentary to aid in its decipherment, which he seems never to have written.

After this exordium there is a long section in which Poliziano first recounts the evolution of man from a primitive state of barbarism towards civilized society, which was brought about by the gift of divine poetry, charioteer and mistress of the soul (v. 70). Then, proceeding to a more metaphysical plane, he describes the origin and manifestations of the divine frenzy that possesses the hearts of men and stirs them to sublime utterances. This whole passage concerning the *furor poeticus* is evidently of Platonic and Neoplatonic inspiration, reflecting the ideas expressed in Plato's *Ion* as well as Ficino's famous epistle entitled *De divino furore* ("On Divine Madness"), his dialogue *De amore* ("On Love") and Book XIII of his *Platonic Theology*. Yet the language is more reminiscent of Ficino's nemesis Lucretius — a good example, once again, of Poliziano's ability to harmonize disparate texts and ideas. In his conception the poet's voice is joined to the cosmic harmony of the spheres, and by a sort of sacred contagion his emotions are transferred to the listener and to future generations of poets.

From this lofty discussion the Tuscan poet turns to a catalogue of poets, beginning with mythical figures, the Sibyls of old — the oracles and prophets of ancient Greece — and the Hebrew prophets, and culminating in the primeval poet Orpheus, his cruel death at the hands of the Bacchantes, and the lurid sequel to his death. It is natural that Poliziano should dwell at some length on the myth of Orpheus, one that was dear to him, and which formed the subject of his play, the *Fabula di Orfeo*. The list of mythical poets continues until we arrive at Homer and the epic genre, in which Poliziano includes poets who wrote in hexameters but not necessarily on epic themes. He spends much time discussing the lives of the poets, drawing on information from a great variety of sources. In this regard a very illuminating document was brought to light some years ago by Lucia Cesarini Martinelli,[4] a notebook of excerpts on the theme of poetry and individual poets that Poliziano compiled just before setting out for the North in the winter of 1479–80. It consists mostly of passages from the Eusebius–Jerome *Chronicon*, the *Lives of Eminent Philosophers* of Diogenes Laertius (partly in Greek and partly in his own Latin paraphrase), Pausanias' *Description of Greece*, various anonymous lives of the poets, the *Moral Essays* of Plutarch, and, among modern works, Book XIV of Boccaccio's *Genealogy of the Pagan Gods*, which contains a debate on the nature of poetry. It is a fascinating find that provides great insight into the creative process in this type of learned, eclectic poetry.

The exhaustive catalogue of poets of both Greece and Rome, some of them shadowy figures, is a kind of poetized version of a famous comparison of Greek and Roman writers made by Quintilian in Book x of the *Institutiones oratoriae*. There are also a few borrowings from a list given by Ovid in an elegy written during the latter's exile on the Black Sea (*Epistulae ex Ponto* 4.16). Of more significance is the tenth poem of Petrarch's *Bucolicum Carmen*, "Laurea occidens" ("The Dying Laurel"), which is also a survey of ancient poets, presented as a journey through the world of the protagonist Silvanus, alias Petrarch, to meet the ancient poets, including Christian poets. Unfortunately, the important tenth book was lacking from Petrarch's copy of Quintilian and, of course, he knew almost no Greek, with the result that Poliziano is obliged to correct silently many misapprehensions in his predecessor.

Proceeding by genres, the inventory enumerates the elegiac poets; bucolic poets; the nine Greek lyric poets traditionally regarded as the most famous representatives of the genre; Latin lyric poetry, including satire; tragedy and comedy both Greek and Latin; mime and other minor genres. It is no jejune catalogue but a brilliant synthesis echoing passages from all periods and forging thematic links from one poet to another. He ends the poem with a delicate homage to Lorenzo's skill in poetic improvisation, inspired in him by a nymph in his retreat at Vallombrosa, and subtly translates into Latin themes and lines of various poetic works of *il Magnifico*. The last part of the poem is reserved for poets in the vernacular tongue: Dante, Petrarch, Boccaccio, Cavalcanti and Lorenzo himself, successors to the great pageant of pagan writers passed in review.

After the publication of the Latin works by Aldo in 1498 the *Silvae* drew the attention of humanist scholars in other countries. In 1513 Nicole Bérault, friend of Budé and Erasmus and teacher at Paris, lectured publicly on the *Rusticus* at the Collège Tréguier in Paris. The text with a commentary was printed anonymously in Paris around 1514, and again around 1518 by Josse Bade. In that same year they were reprinted by Froben in Basel. In his *praelectio* to his commentary Froben states that Poliziano is not only to be compared but even preferred to many of the ancient writers.

In Germany the *Rusticus* with the commentary of Johann Murmelling (Murmellius) was published in Münster in 1510. Another German scholar, Johann Ludwig Kohlbürger (known as Brassicanus), published the *Nutricia* with an ample commentary at Nuremberg in 1514. The famous Spanish humanist, Francisco Sánchez, called El Brocense from the town of Las Brozas in Estremadura, published all four *Silvae* with extensive scholia in Salamanca, 1554,[5] and it was republished again in Salamanca in 1596. Recently, an uncatalogued book of the British Library has been identified as an edition of the *Silvae*. The type would indicate that it was printed by the famous printer of the Polyglot Complutensian Bible, Arnao Guillén de Brocar, and the date of publication is conjectured as *ca.* 1515–1520.[6]

I am supremely grateful to my good friend and fellow translator of Erasmus' *Correspondence*, Alexander Dalzell, a superb Latinist and, in particular, a connoisseur of Latin didactic poetry, for his scrupulous reading of the translation, to which he made many elegant and timely improvements. To James Hankins, indefatigable advocate and editor of the whole enterprise, I express my warm thanks for his encouragement and adroit refinements to the writing, executed with his customary exquisite critical acumen. I should like also to express my sincere gratitude to W. Keats Sparrow, Dean of the Harriot College of Arts and Sciences at East Carolina University, for his sedulous support of humane letters, which provides me with great incentive for my own scholarly pursuits. I wish devoutly to dedicate this book to the beloved memory of Sydney Diane Lane.

NOTES

1. Angelo Poliziano, *Miscellaneorum Centuria Prima*, ed. H. Katayama (Tokyo: University of Tokyo Press, 1982), p. 352.

2. Tacitus, *Dialogus de oratoribus* 2.18, quoted in *Oratio super Fabio Quintiliano et Statii Sylvis* in *Prosatori latini del Quattrocento*, ed. Eugenio Garin (Naples-Milan: Ricciardi, 1952), p. 878.

3. It should be noted that Poliziano usually adopts the spelling *Sylvae* in referring to Statius' work, but the title of his own poems beginning with the second editions is *Silvae*.

4. Lucia Cesarini Martinelli, "'De poesi et poetis': Uno schedario sconosciuto di Angelo Poliziano," in *Tradizione classica e letteratura umanistica: Per Alessandro Perosa*, ed. R. Cardini, E. Garin, L. Cesarini Martinelli, G. Pascucci, vol. 2 (Rome: Bulzoni, 1985), pp. 455–487.

5. *Silvae, poema quidem obscurum sed novis nunc scholiis illustratum per Franciscum Sanctium Brocensem.*

6. Cf. Dennis E. Rhodes, "An Unrecognized Spanish Edition of Poliziano's *Silvae*," *British Library Journal* 15 (1989): 208–211.

SILVAE

MANTO

Angelus Politianus Laurentio Petri Francisci filio Medici S. D.

Cogis tu quidem me, Laurenti, carmen edere inconditum, inemen-
datum, et quod in publico semel pronuntiatum, nimis fuisse im-
pudens visum sit. Satis profecto fuerat vixisse unum diem quod
tam foret imperfectum animal, ac posse etiam inter insecta illa
quae vocentur ephemera connumerari. Namque ego id ad praesen-
tem dumtaxat celebritatem, quasi Adonidos hortum, concinnave-
ram. Prorogare tu nostrae *Mantus* (ita enim inscribimus) non tam
vitam cupis quam dedecus. Ferreus sim si tibi quid denegem, tam
nobili adulescenti, tam probo, tam mei amanti, tanto denique eam
rem studio efflagitanti. Quare habe tibi quidquid hoc libelli, ac
tu quoque desiderio nostro aliquando subveni; et quae tibi Mu-
sae amatoria carmina vernaculae suggerunt, ne patere, quaeso, a
nobis expectari diutius. Vale. Florentiae, IV nonas Novembres
MCCCCLXXXII.

MANTO

Angelo Poliziano to Lorenzo, son of Pierfrancesco de' Medici,[1] greeting.

You compel me, Lorenzo, to publish an unpolished, uncorrected poem; even to have recited it once in public would have seemed too shameless. Surely it would have been enough that such an imperfect creature, which might be numbered among those insects called ephemera,[2] should have lived but for a day. For I had put it together merely for a specific occasion, like a garden of Adonis.[3] You wish to prolong not so much the life as the disgrace of our *Manto* (for so did we entitle it). I should be hard-hearted if I denied anything to you, such a noble young man, so virtuous, so devoted to me, and finally so insistent in your demands. Therefore, accept this little book, whatever its worth, and for your part satisfy at long last a desire of mine: do not keep me waiting any longer, I pray you, for those love lyrics which the vernacular Muses supply. Farewell. Florence, 2 November 1482.

Stabat adhuc rudibus Pagaseo in litore remis
    quae ratis undosum prima cucurrit iter.
Dum tamen extremis haerent succincta ceruchis
    lintea, dum nautas flamina nulla vocant,
5   conveniunt Minyae gemini Chironis ad antrum,
    qua fugit obliquo garrula lympha pede,
quaque ingens platanus genialibus excubat umbris;
    explicat hic faciles rustica mensa dapes.
Crescit fronde torus, vernant in flore capilli,
10   sed viret Herculeis populus alba comis.
Dat puer Aeacides nivea carchesia dextra,
    sed suus Alcidae pocula miscet Hylas.
Finis erat dapibus; citharam pius excitat Orpheus
    et movet ad doctas verba canora manus.
15   Conticuere viri, tenuere silentia venti,
    vosque retro cursum mox tenuistis, aquae;
iam volucres fessis pendere sub aethera pinnis,
    iamque truces videas ora tenere feras;
decurrunt scopulis auritae ad carmina quercus
20   nudaque Peliacus culmina motat apex.
Et iam materno permulserat omnia cantu,
    cum tacuit querulam deposuitque fidem.
Occupat hanc audax digitosque affringit Achilles
    indoctumque rudi personat ore puer.
25   Materiam quaeris? Laudabat carmina blandi
    hospitis et tantae murmura magna lyrae.
Riserunt Minyae; sed enim tibi dicitur, Orpheu,
    haec pueri pietas grata fuisse nimis.
Me quoque nunc magni nomen celebrare Maronis
30   (si qua fides vero est) gaudet et ipse Maro.

A Preface to the Silva of Angelo Poliziano
Entitled Manto

It stood there still on the shore of Pagasae,[4] the craft that first crossed the waves, its oars yet untried. But while the furled sails remain fastened to the yard-arms, while no breezes invite the sailors, the Minyans[5] gather at the cave of biformed Chiron,[6] where the gurgling stream rushes by along its oblique path and the towering plane-tree stands guard with friendly shade; here a rustic table provides a simple banquet. A leafy bower is erected, they adorn their hair with spring flowers, but Hercules' locks gleam with the leaves of the white poplar. The boy Achilles distributes drinking cups with his immaculate hand, while Hylas[7] mixes the wine and water for his companion Hercules. When the meal is ended, faithful Orpheus stirs his lyre and his skillful fingers accompany the tuneful song. The men fell silent and the winds were still, and you, O waters, promptly reversed your course. Now you could see the birds hang suspended in the air on their tired wings, and ravenous beasts closed their gaping jaws; the oaks give ear and rush down from the cliffs, and the peak of Mount Pelion shakes its bare summits. And now he had charmed all things with his maternal song when suddenly he broke off and set down his plaintive lyre. Boldly Achilles takes it up and rubs his fingers upon it, and the young boy sings an unpolished tune in his untrained voice. Do you ask what was his theme? He praised the songs of his charming host and the sublime music of his great lyre. The Minyans laughed, but it is said that you, Orpheus, were more than pleased with the young boy's show of devotion. Even Maro himself will be glad, if we may presume it to be true, that I, too, am celebrating the name of the great Maro.[8]

Angeli Politiani silva in Bucolicon
Vergili enarratione pronuntiata

Est dea quae vacuo sublimis in aere pendens
it nimbo succincta latus, sed candida pallam,
sed radiata comam ac stridentibus insonat alis.
Haec spes immodicas premit, haec infesta superbis
5   imminet, huic celsas hominum contundere mentes
successusque datum et nimios turbare paratus,
quam veteres Nemesin, genitam de Nocte silenti
Oceano dixere patri. Stant sidera fronti,
frena manu pateramque gerit; semperque verendum
10   ridet et insanis obstat contraria coeptis,
improba vota domans ac summis ima revolvens,
miscet et alterna nostros vice temperat actus
atque huc atque illuc ventorum turbine fertur.
Viderat haec domitis tumidam te, Graecia, Persis,
15   signa quoque Eoum victricia ferre sub orbem;
viderat et cantu Aonio eloquiisque superbam
ire altum magnumque loqui caeloque supinum
insertare caput nec dis te ferre minorem.
Mox fastus exosa graves, cervice coegit
20   ferre iugum et Latiis superatam subdidit armis.
Nec fandi permansit honos: tu namque potenti
protinus ore tonans, ardentis fulmine linguae
cuncta quatis, Cicero; Pyliae non mella senectae
nec iam Dulichias audet conferre procellas,
25   sponte tibi virides transcribens Graecia palmas.
Se tamen Aoniae solatur fronde coronae:
deerat adhuc Latio vatum decus, horrida quamquam
bella tubasque rudi cantaverat Ennius arte.

A Silva of Angelo Poliziano Recited as an Introduction to Lectures on the Bucolics of Vergil

There is a goddess suspended on high upon the vacant air who makes her way girded by a cloud, but her mantle is of a brilliant white, her hair radiant, and her whirring wings produce a shrill sound. She suppresses immoderate hopes and fiercely menaces the proud; it was given to her to crush the haughty minds of men and to rout their successes and their ambitious projects. The ancients called her Nemesis,[9] born of the silent night to Ocean, her father. Stars adorn her brow; in her hand she holds the bridle and the libation bowl; she ceases not to utter a fearsome laugh and she stands opposed to senseless undertakings, quelling evil desires. And turning everything topsy-turvy, she confounds and orders our actions by turns and is borne hither and thither by the force of the whirlwind. She saw you, Greece, swollen with pride after your defeat of the Persians, carrying your victorious standards to the lands of the East. She saw you, too, proud of your Aonian[10] song and of your eloquence, exalted and grandiloquent, lifting your head to touch the skies, and thinking you were not less than the gods. Then, detesting your excessive pride, she forced you to bear the yoke upon your neck and subjected you in inglorious defeat to the might of Latin arms. Nor even did the honor of eloquence remain; for you, Cicero, thundering forth with powerful voice and with the lightning bolt of your blazing tongue, make all things tremble. Greece does not dare to compare the honeyed words of the old king of Pylos[11] nor the stormy eloquence of Ulysses to you, conferring voluntarily upon you the green palm of victory. Yet it consoles itself with the leafy garland of the Muses: the glory of poets was yet lacking to Latium, although Ennius[12] had sung of horrid wars and the blaring trumpet with his rough-hewn skill. Be-

Editus ecce Maro, quo non felicior alter,
30 seu silvas seu rura canit sive arma virumque;
    namque Syracosiis cum vix assurgat avenis,
    Hesiodum premit et magno contendit Homero.
    Ergo age, quis centum mihi nunc in carmina linguas
    immensumque loqui vocemque effundere aenam,
35 quis mihi det Siculas Latio clangore sorores
    post Geticam superare chelyn, dum te, optime vatum,
    imbellis pietas audaci promere cantu
    audet Atlanteasque humeris fulcire columnas?
    Unde ego tantarum repetam primordia laudum?
40 Aut qua fine sequar? Facit ingens copia rerum
    incertum. Sic frondifera lignator in Ida
    stat dubius, vastae quae primum robora silvae
    vulneret: hinc patulam procero stipite fagum,
    hic videt annosam sua pandere bracchia quercum,
45 illic succinctas caput exsertare cupressos
    metiturque oculis Phrygiae nemora alta parentis.
        Te nascente, Maro, Parnassi e culmine summo
    adfuit Aonias inter festina sorores
    Calliope, blandisque exceptum sustulit ulnis
50 permulsitque manu quatiens terque oscula iunxit;
    omina ter cecinit, ter lauro tempora cinxit.
    Mox aliae dant quaeque tuis munuscula cunis:
    certatim dant plectra, lyram, pellemque pedumque,
    dant et multiforam modulanda ad carmina loton
55 et decrescenti compactas ordine avenas,
    dant Pandionias volucres; ter murmure placant
    liventes oculos, ter frontem baccare tangunt.
    Venit et Elysio venturi praescia Manto,
    Manto quae iuvenem fluvio conceperat Ocnum,
60 Ocnum qui matris dederat tibi, Mantua, nomen.

8

hold! Maro was born, with whom none can compare, whether he
sing of woodlands or countryside or "arms and the man," for
though he barely rivals the Syracusan piper,[13] he surpasses Hesiod
and contends with great Homer. Therefore, come now, who will
give me a hundred tongues for my songs, who will give me an un-
bounded eloquence, a voice of bronze? Who will give me the
power to outdo the Sicilian sisters[14] with a Latin trumpet blast af-
ter the Thracian lyre,[15] while my unwarlike devotion dares to cele-
brate you, O prince of poets, in an audacious song, and support
the pillars of Atlas on my shoulders? Where shall I begin to sing
his praises? Or where shall I end? The abundance of material
makes me uncertain. Thus does the woodcutter on leafy Mt. Ida[16]
stand undecided about which tree of the vast forest he will first
strike down: here he sees a spreading beech rising on its towering
trunk, here he sees an aged oak stretching out its branches, there
he sees the bushy-topped pines reaching into the sky; and with his
eyes he scans the deep groves of the Phrygian mother.

At your birth, Maro, Calliope[17] left the heights of Parnassus,
hastening to join her sister Muses, and she took you into her ten-
der arms and cradling you, she caressed you and kissed you three
times; three times she chanted prophecies and three times she
wreathed your temples with laurel. Then the others competed
with one another to offer tiny gifts at your cradle: they give you
a plectrum, a lyre, a fleece and a crook; they give you also a lo-
tus flute with many holes to fashion songs, and oaten pipes ar-
ranged in diminishing order of length; they give you the birds of
Pandion,[18] three times they placate envious eyes with gentle whis-
pers, three times they touch your brow with baccharis.[19] From
Elysium comes also Manto,[20] who knows the future, Manto who
had conceived the young Ocnus in a river, Ocnus who gave to you,
Mantua, his mother's name. She comes, and shaking her head-
band and her disheveled locks, and rolling her bloodshot eyes,

Venit, et horrentes quatiens vittamque comasque
sanguineamque rotans aciem, sic ora resolvit
plena deo et veras excussit pectore voces:
    'Dicebam, memini, memini, tibi, Mantua, quondam:
65   "Surge, bonis avibus fundata et fulmine laevo,
surge paremque astris contende educere molem
pyramidum supra sumptus. Pro quanta manet te
gloria! quam longum senibus celebrabere saeclis!
Nascetur, video, supera tibi missus ab arce
70   sidereus vates, alti cui numinis haustum
mens caelo cognata ferat, quem grande sonantem
non Linus Inachides tantum atque Oeagrius Orpheus
aut mea qui Tyrio construxit moenia plectro,
sed vos, o Musae, sed tu mireris, Apollo."
75   Et nunc, ecce puer tranquillae ad limina lucis
ille diu promissus adest vitamque salutans,
has teneris iam nunc mulcet vagitibus auras.
Euge, beate puer, sanguis meus! Horreat ortus
Graecia tota tuos laurumque habitura secundam
80   Ascra, Arethusa suis metuant et Smyrna coronis.'
    Incipe adhuc gracili connectere carmina filo,
incipe, magne puer; nec vota intexere Diris
impia, nec culici gemitum praestare merenti,
nec te Lampsacium pudeat lusisse Ithyphallum
85   blandaque lascivis epigrammata pingere chartis.
Acmonidas refer et Brontem Volcaniaque antra
ignivomosque apices montis raucoque trementem
murmure Trinacriam, quoties per nubila flammas
eructat tentatque latus versare Typhoeus.
90   Dic Scyllam subitis miseram quae se induit alis,
Scyllam quae nimio flagrans Minois amore
ah! potuit rigido genitorem invadere ferro
crudelis, potuit cano spoliare capillo

filled with the god, she opens her mouth and utters these veridical words:

"I remember, I remember that I used to say to you, O Mantua, long ago: 'Rise up, you who were founded with a good omen of birds and lightning on the left; rise up and strive to raise an edifice 65 that will reach the stars, greater than the splendor of the pyramids. Oh! what great glory awaits you! How long you will be celebrated in centuries to come! There will be born, I see it, a heavenly poet, sent down from the citadel of heaven, whose mind, divine by nature, will give him a draught of the divine essence, 70 whose magniloquence will be admired not only by Linus,[21] descendant of Inachus, and Orpheus, son of Oeagrus, or the one who built the walls of my city by the power of his Tyrian plectrum,[22] but by you, Muses, and by you, Apollo.' And now, behold! That long-promised child is here at the threshold of serene light, 75 and greeting life, he already beguiles the breezes with his tender wailings. Bravo, blessed child, my blood! May all of Greece shudder at your birth, and may Ascra, Arethusa and Smyrna,[23] destined to hold second place, fear for their crowns." 80

Begin to fashion your poems[24] with a thread still fine; begin, great child; do not be ashamed to weave impious imprecations to the Furies or to have a deserving gnat pour forth just laments, or to write an amusing poem about an Ithyphallus[25] of Lampsacus, or to sketch charming epigrams in lascivious pages. Tell of the 85 sons of Acmon and Brontes[26] and the caves of Vulcan, and the mountain peaks that belch forth fire, and Trinacria[27] trembling with raucous rumblings whenever Typhoeus[28] discharges flames through the clouds and turns over on his side; tell of unhappy Scylla, who suddenly sprouted wings, Scylla,[29] who, burning with 90 inordinate love for Minos, oh! had the courage to set upon her father with the unyielding sword and cruelly cut off his white hair,

crudelis — sed quis duro contendat Amori?
95 Crudelis, sed culpa tua est, tua culpa, Cupido.
Atque haec prima novi fuerint elementa poetae,
haec fuerint timidae praeludia prima iuventae.
Iam vatem, iam, Roma, vocas; iam saeva recessit
paupertas praestatque piis grata otia Musis
100 Tuscus eques. Nosco hunc, atavis qui regibus ortus,
discinctum iuvenem; cerno et te, maxime princeps,
purpureos inter proceres sanctumque senatum
pendentem stare ad numeros atque ora tenentem.
Tu, tamen, o miserae nimium vicina Cremonae,
105 quid fles amissum, quid fles, mea Mantua, campum
pascentem niveos herboso flumine cycnos?
Nonne vides, ingrata, tuis quae praemia damnis
accumulent superi et solatia quanta rependant?
Ipsa en Roma tuo sese quoque iactat alumno.
110 Iamque Phalantei resonant pineta Galaesi,
Tityre, te vacuo meditantem murmur in antro,
iamque tuam dociles recinunt Amaryllida silvae.
Nigraque dum raucum tremulis evibrat ab alis
carmen et epoto canit ebria rore cicada,
115 montibus ah! solis formosum iactat Alexin
vocalis Corydon et "Alexin" reddit imago.
Ecce autem imparibus dum sibila flectit avenis
impubis pastor, faciles dum ludit amores,
aureolo petit hunc malo lascivaque currit
120 ad salices nymphe furtivo prodita risu.
Sed maiora vocant; nunc, o nunc omnis abesto
impius et casti linguisque animisque favento:
stelligero Deus ille, Deus se fundit ab axe,
aeterni mens certa Patris quique omnia nutu
125 torquet Idumaeae se virginis inserit alvo,
aurea sparsurus redivivo saecula mundo.

cruel one; but who can contend with pitiless Love? Cruel was she, but it is your fault, Cupid, your fault. And these will be the first 95 beginnings of the new poet, these will be the first preludes of timorous youth. Already, Rome, you summon the poet; already harsh poverty has withdrawn and the Etruscan knight[30] provides the leisure agreeable to the sacred Muses. I recognize this young man in 100 his loose-fitting tunic, who sprang from ancient kings; I see you also, most great prince,[31] standing among the purple-clad nobles and the venerable Senate, listening attentively to his verse and fixing your gaze upon him. But you, my beloved Mantua, too close to unfortunate Cremona,[32] why do you weep over the lost fields that pasture the snow-white swans with their grassy stream? Do 105 you not see, ungrateful one, what compensations the gods award you for your losses and with what consolations they repay you? Behold, Rome itself boasts of your son.

And now the pine groves of the Galaesus[33] in Tarentum re-echo 110 the plaintive strain,[34] Tityrus, which you improvise in a deserted grotto, and the woods, eager to learn, resound with the name of Amaryllis. And while the black cicada emits its shrill sound with the vibrations of its wings and intoxicated with the dew sings its song, sweet-tongued Corydon boasts of the beautiful Alexis, ah! upon the solitary mountainside and the echo repeats "Alexis." Be- 115 hold, while the beardless shepherd modulates the sibilant sounds on his uneven pipes, while he idles away his time, singing of casual love affairs, a playful nymph throws a golden apple at him and then runs to the willow trees, betrayed by her furtive laughter. But 120 greater themes beckon; now, O now let every profane person stay away and let the chaste-minded abstain from any ill-omened word or thought: the great god rushes down from the starry sky,[35] the unchanging mind of the eternal Father, who sets all things in motion with a simple nod of his head; he encloses himself within the womb of a virgin of Idumea[36] to bring back the Golden Age to a 125 rejuvenated world.

Tu tamen ante alios felix, mea vera propago,
cui licitum in silvis inter coryleta iacenti
rimari quid fata parent, quid pulchra minentur
130   sidera, quique mihi divini pectoris haeres,
enthea Cumaeis incingas tempora vittis.
Verum age iam, gelidosque tegant umbracula fontes
et foliis cumuletur humus, densique maniplis
inspirent flores vacuoque incisa sepulchro
135   candida formosum testetur littera Daphnin,
Daphnin ad astra vocet tenero cava fistula cantu.
Ebrius interea nostri nutritor Iacchi
Silenus molli dormit resupinus in antro,
ebrius et nimio venas tumefactus alumno;
140   securum pueri audaces atque improba nais
invadunt furtim deque ipsis vincla coronis,
quae senis e mutilo modo vertice defluxerunt,
iniiciunt alacres promissaque carmina poscunt,
carmina cum silvis totos mulcentia montes.
145   Iamque tuis, Minci, glauca sub harundine ripis
vincitur alterno Corydonis carmine Thyrsis;
iam repetit querulam Damonis tibia Musam,
Damonis Musam scopuli pinusque loquuntur.
Sed quid, io, tam dulce tibi est, Galatea, sub undis,
150   quam formosa vocet nequiquam ad litora Cyclops?
Infelix Cyclops! Sed enim infelicior illo
Gallus amat queriturque suam procul esse Lycorin,
Gallus, quem rigidae flevere in montibus orni,
cuius amorem omnes nequeunt mutare labores;
155   Gallus, quem frustra verbis solatus Apollo est.
Haec sat erit simas inter cecinisse capellas
pastorem. Tu victricem fer, Mantua, palmam.
    Ecce lacertosi quaerunt nova turba coloni
quo segetes veniant campo, quo sidere tellus

But you are blessed above all others, you, my true progeny, to whom it was granted, lying in the woods among the hazel-thickets, to examine what the fates are preparing, what the beautiful stars are threatening; may you, the heir of my divine spirit, bind   130
your inspired temples with the bands of the Cumean prophetess. But come, may the shady foliage cover the icy springs, and may the ground be covered with leaves, and may the flowers gathered in bouquets emanate their perfume and may the clear letters inscribed on the empty tomb proclaim the beautiful Daphnis, and   135
may the hollow reed trumpet his name to the stars with its gentle song. Meanwhile drunken Silenus,[37] who brought up our Bacchus, sleeps reclining in a pleasant cave, drunk, his veins bursting with wine. Daring youths and a shameless nymph sneak up on him, all   140
unaware, and swiftly they tie him up with bonds made of the very wreaths that have just slipped from the old man's bald head, and they demand the promised songs, songs that delight the mountains and the woodlands. And already on your banks, O Mincius,[38] covered with blue-grey reeds, Thyrsis is bested in his   145
amoebean singing contest with Corydon. Already the reed-pipe of Damon repeats its plaintive Muse; the rocks and the pines resound with Damon's Muse. But what is it, Galatea,[39] that you find so sweet under the waves, when Cyclops invites you in vain to the lovely shores? Poor Cyclops! But Gallus is more unlucky than   150
he in love, and laments that his beloved Lycoris is far away — Gallus,[40] for whom the unbending ash trees wept upon the mountains, whose love cannot be changed despite all his efforts; Gallus, whom Apollo tried to solace in vain with his words. These strains,   155
divine Muses, it will be enough for your shepherd to have sung among the snub-nosed goats. You Mantua, bear off the palm of victory!

Behold a new throng, brawny farmers,[41] seek to know in what fields their crops will prosper, under what star the land should be

160   vertatur, quod sit falcis, quod tempus aratri.
Egredere o silvis, iuvenis, curruque levatus
Triptolemi, Latios fecunda messibus agros.
Nec caelebs iam palmes agat, sed reptet ad ulmum
ebrius at dulci rubeat nova nupta marito;

165   et pater Autumnus medio consurgat ab arvo
pomiferum viridi caput alte umbratus amictu
atque, Acheloe, tuum teneat grave dextera cornu
stetque catenatas suadens nudare palaestras
Palladis ampla arbos bicoloribus horrida baccis

170   frondibus et versis longum discriminet annum.
Iam laetos inter saltus frondosaque tesqua
hinc vitulus primo cui frons protuberet aevo
mugitu tenero matrem vocet, inde per herbas
candida lascivo discurrat bucula saltu.

175   At quibus assurgunt pleno iam cornua gyro
inter se adverso decertent pectore amantes,
dum rudis exultim florentis in aequore campi
ludit equus volucresque fuga praevertere ventos
aut tranare amnes aut cursu evincere montem

180   gestit, Olympiacae rapturus dona coronae.
Lanigerumque pecus primo propellat Eoo
de stabulis pastor, dum pratis roscida lucent
gramina, dum teretes per flexa cacumina guttae
colludunt; ipsae haerentes vix rupibus altis

185   aspera Cinyphiae carpant dumeta capellae.
Tum glomerata cavo fundant se examina saxo
halantemque rosam et tenerorum germina florum
taurigenae populentur apes plenoque recurrant
poplite; iam lentum teneat fundamina gluten,

190   iam portas arcemque et propugnacula condant
ceraque nectareas ducat sexangula cellas;
aut natos aut mella legant fucosque repellant,

ploughed, what is the time for the sickle and what the time for the 160
plough. Emerge from the woods, young man, and raising yourself
up on the chariot of Triptolemus,[42] make the fields of Latium rich
with harvests. The vine-shoot must not remain unwed but creep
along to the elm, drunk, and blush like a newly-wed before her
dear spouse. And may father Autumn rise up from the midst of
the ploughed field, his pomiferous head cloaked in a green mantle; 165
and, Acheloüs,[43] may your right hand bear the copious horn; and
may the stout tree of Pallas, thick with bi-colored olives, stand
forth and urge on the youths, baring their bodies, to engage in in-
terlocked combat; and by inverting its leaves[44] may it divide the
long year in two parts. Now amidst the lush pastures and the 170
wooded thickets let the calf, whose brow is sprouting its first
horns, call to its mother in a soft lowing sound and let the white
heifer bound over the meadows with frolicsome step.

But let the young bulls, whose horns have grown full circle, 175
contend with one another, breast to breast, in the contests of love,
while the untamed horse cavorts in the level expanse of the flow-
ering fields and is anxious to outstrip the swift winds in flight or
swim across rivers or race over the mountains, destined one day to
carry away the Olympic prize. Let the shepherd drive his woolly 180
flock from the fold at break of dawn, while the dewy grass gleams
on the meadows, while the round droplets sport on the drooping
stalks; let the Cinyphian goats,[45] barely clinging to the high crags,
crop the thorny bushes. Then let the dense swarms rush forth 185
from the hollow rock and let the bees, generated from an ox,[46] pil-
lage the fragrant rose and the buds of delicate flowers and return,
their legs laden with pollen; may a viscous glue now hold together
the foundations of the comb; may they now construct the doors,
the citadel and the ramparts, and may the wax shape the hexago- 190
nal cells that will receive the nectar; let them gather their young
and the honey; let them drive away the drones, a loathsome breed

turpe pecus, iamque accinctae civilibus armis
expediantque manus rostris et spicula vibrent
195 nocturnoque sonent mussantia castra susurro.
At tu, quae tellus aestuque geluque laboras,
cui sacer hibernos Helicon intercipit ortus,
ne cessa acceptam nostrae submittere laurum.
   Nec iam supremi certent de sanguine vatis
200 Smyrna Rhodos Colophon Salamis Chios Argos Athenae,
quippe Bianoream manet haec victoria gentem.
Namque meus timido qui rura et pascua versu
hactenus excoluit, stimulis tandem acribus actus
dediscetque metum validasque in pectora vires
205 contrahet attonitoque canet fera pectine bella.
Qualis adhuc brevibus quae vix bene fidere pinnis
coepit avis, matrem primo nidosque loquaces
circumit et crebrum patula super arbore sidit;
colligit inde animos sensim et vicina volatu
210 stagna legit terrasque capit captasque relinquit
lascivitque fuga; tandem et sublimia tranat
nubila et iratis audens se credere ventis,
in spatia excurrit iustisque eremigat alis.
   Ac primum Siculis magnum producet ab oris
215 Laomedontiaden undisque et turbine saevo
auferet in Libyen, quem Dido ignara futuri
(sic placitum superis) animoque domoque receptet.
Reginaeque hospes diri commenta Sinonis,
mendaces Graios, vanae periuria gentis
220 et populata malis Neptunia Pergama flammis,
se quoque iactatum referet terraque marique;
illa avidis bibet ignem oculis noctemque diemque
nutriet infelix vesanum pectore amorem.
Venatu tandem in medio Saturnia nimbum
225 pronuba diffundet soloque Hymenaeus in antro

and, prepared for civil strife, let them make ready their troops with pointed snouts, and let them brandish their stings; let the humming camps resound with nocturnal murmurs. But you, a land that suffers both heat and cold, from whom sacred Helicon[47] cuts off the winter sun, do not hesitate to submit the laurel you have received to ours. 195

May Smyrna, Rhodes, Colophon, Salamis, Chios, Argos and Athens[48] dispute the birthplace of the supreme poet no more, because this victory now belongs to the race of Bianor.[49] For my descendant, who until now has sung in modest verse of countryside and pastures, driven now by strong incentives, will put aside all fear and, mustering mighty strength in his heart, will sing of cruel wars on his inspired lyre. Just so a fledgling that begins slowly to trust its short feathers, at first flies around its mother and the chirping nests and frequently rests on the branches of the wide spreading tree, then little by little takes courage and skims over the nearby ponds in flight, then reaches land and instantly leaves it behind, delighting in its speed; at length it traverses the clouds on high and, daring to entrust itself to the angry winds, journeys into space and navigates on sure wings. 200 205 210

And first he shall lead the great descendant of Laomedon[50] from the shores of Sicily and through the waves and the fierce storm he will take him to Libya, where Dido, ignorant of the future (so it pleased the gods), will accept him into her heart and into her palace. The guest will tell the queen of the fabrications of treacherous Sinon,[51] the lying Greeks, the perjuries of that perfidious race, and Neptunian Pergamum,[52] laid waste by the destructive flames, and how he was tossed on land and sea; she will drink in the fire of love with avid eyes, and day and night the tragic queen will nourish the insane passion in her breast. Finally, in the midst of the hunt the daughter of Saturn,[53] as *pronuba*,[54] will unleash a storm and Hymen[55] will be present in the solitary cave, but (gloomy omen!) will not bring any torches. The upper 215 220 225

adfuerit; nullasque faces, maestum, afferet, omen!
fulgoresque dabit, nymphis ululantibus, aether.
Ipse Iovis monitu Aeneas rursum ire per undas
cogetur vento, rursum Itala quaerere regna,
230   surgentem Ausoniae solio impositurus Iulum.
At Phoenissa rogum saevo furiata dolore
inscendet moritura trucesque in vota vocabit
Eumenidas; mox et Phrygium, pro tristia dona,
ah! niveum per pectus aget miserabilis ensem.
235   Discolor interea taurino combibet ore
Iris aquas iterumque antris effundet apertis
Hippotades hiemem et rapidis ruet aequora ventis.
Zanclaeas iterum fessi eiicientur ad oras
Troes et hospito fidi accipientur Acestae;
240   hic patris ad tumulum sollemnes ordine pompas
dux feret ac meritos celebrabit litore ludos.
Tum pelagus relegens, amisso praeside puppis,
vix tandem Euboica lacrimans potietur harena.
Atque ubi fata deum vivacis ab ore Sibyllae
245   hauserit, infernas etiam descendet ad umbras,
o pietas! manesque petet per Averna paternos
Romanosque suos Lethaei ad fluminis undam
conferet et magnos gaudens cognoscet Iulos
paciferumque ducem fulvo cui pulchra metallo
250   saecla fluent, cui pressa gravi pede bella iacebunt.
His laetus porta ad socios evadet eburna
dux Anchisiades Tuscumque enabit ad amnem.
Necdum parta quies: restant bella aspera, restant,
et crassus multo stagnabit funere Tibris.
255   At tibi Castaliis renoventur pectora lymphis,
care nepos; nunc, nunc ingenti est ore sonandum.
Grande opus a tergo, quis enim alto evincere cantu
clamoresque virum atque hinnitus speret equorum?

air will send forth lightning as the nymphs howl. Aeneas himself
at the command of Jupiter will be forced to put to sea again at the
mercy of the wind and again seek the kingdom of Italy, to place
the young Iulus[56] on the throne of Ausonia.[57] But the Phoenician,   230
driven mad by her cruel sorrow, will ascend the pyre to seek her
death and will call upon the pitiless Furies to hear her maledic-
tions; then the ill-starred queen will plunge the Phrygian sword,
alas! fatal gift, into her snow-white bosom. In the meanwhile
multi-colored Iris[58] with her taurine visage will drink up the wa-   235
ters, and once again the son of Hippotes[59] will let loose a storm
from the unbarred caves and will swoop down on the seas with
turbulent winds. Again the weary Trojans will be cast upon the
Zanclean shores[60] and will be welcomed by the hospitality of
faithful Acestes.[61] Here the leader will inaugurate solemn rites at
the tomb of his father and celebrate the appropriate games on the   240
shore. Then returning to the sea, after losing the ship's pilot,[62] in
tears and with great difficulty he will reach the Euboean shore.[63]
And after he has heard the fates willed by the gods from the lips
of the long-lived Sibyl, he will descend even to the infernal shades
(O what filial devotion!) and will seek his father's spirit in the   245
realm of Avernus.[64] He will pass in review his Roman descendants
near the waters of the river Lethe[65] and will have the pleasure
of meeting the Julian line and the peace-bringing prince, under
whom the age, embellished by golden metal, will return, and at
whose coming wars will lie prostrate, crushed under his weighty
foot. Made happy by these tidings, the warrior son of Anchises   250
will ascend to his companions through the ivory gate and sail to
the Etruscan river. Peace has not yet been attained; harsh wars re-
main and the turbid Tiber will be clogged with mass slaughter.
But may your heart be restored by the waters of Castalia,[66] dear   255
descendant; now, now a heroic song must be sung. A great work
presses on you, for who can hope to equal in lofty song the cries of
heroes and the neighing of horses? But you will succeed; it is given

Tu tamen evinces; licitum tibi, maxime vatum,
260   arma, acies, furias, Martem ipsum aequare canendo.
Iamque volans superas Alecto impune per auras
Tartareum canit et resides stridentibus hydris
instimulat; dux ipsa manu Saturnia saeva
claustra quatit belli postesque irata refringit.
265   Iam Latiae coiere manus, domat aspera duris
ora lupis sonipes facilesque in pulvere gyros
flectit eques; ipsae alpino de vertice silvae
praecipitant, avidae Phrygios haurire cruores;
iam rastri pondus rigidum diffingit in ensem
270   caedis amor versique abeunt in pila ligones
attritusque cava mutatur casside vomis;
iamque aurem horrisono rumpunt fera classica bombo
armorumque minax praestringit lumina fulgor.
Dumque alacres secum in Martem Cythereius heros
275   Arcadas et missum auspicio Pallanta sinistro
audacem puerum melioraque fata secutos
Tyrrhenos rapit et tantis accingitur ausis,
ecce furens Rutulus saevoque instinctus amore,
nequiquam in Phrygiam iaculatus lampada classem,
280   miratur subitas pelago consurgere nymphas;
nec minus irrumpit castris altamque cruentus
dat stragem fluvioque evadit laetus amico.
Ultor adest sociosque exponens litore tuto,
auspicium belli, maternis fulgurat armis
285   Dardanides totasque in pugnam exsuscitat iras.
O qui sudor equis! Qui se alto in pulvere reges
turpabunt! Quanto exsurget rubra sanguine tellus!
Nec tuus hasta deus nec te tua dextera forti,
Mezenti, leto eripiet visque effera mentis,
290   sed consors nato accedes tumulique necisque.
At tu quo, nimio spoliorum et laudis amore

to you, greatest of poets, to equal in your singing arms, battle-
lines, mad fury, Mars himself. And now Alecto,[67] flying undis-   260
turbed through the upper air, sounds the infernal signal, and
goads the sluggish with her hissing hydras; the cruel daughter of
Saturn with her own hands makes the temple[68] where war is en-
closed tremble and in her wrath breaks open its door. Now the
Latin forces are assembled; the horse feels the jagged bit in its un-   265
tamed mouth, the horseman executes agile turns in the dust; the
forests themselves rush down headlong from the Alpine peaks, ea-
ger to imbibe Trojan blood. Now the love of bloodshed converts
the heavy drag-hoe into a rigid sword, and mattocks are turned   270
into javelins and the worn ploughshare becomes a hollow helmet.
Now the fierce trumpets break upon the ear with their dreadful
roar and the menacing glitter of armor dazzles the eye. And as
the Cytherean hero[69] carries off with him into battle the eager
Arcadians and Pallas, the courageous youth, sent under a dire   275
omen, and the Etruscans, striving for a better fate, and as he read-
ies himself for such great exploits, behold, the raging Rutulian,[70]
inspired by fierce desire, after hurling torches in vain upon the
Phrygian fleet, is amazed to see nymphs suddenly arise from the
sea. Nonetheless, he bursts into the camp, and stained with blood,   280
spreads carnage far and wide, and joyously escapes, thanks to the
friendly river. The avenging Trojan arrives and, disembarking his
allies on the safe shore, harbinger of war, resplendent in the armor
his mother gave him, he rouses up the anger of his troops for the
fight. O in what sweat the horses are bathed! How the kings will   285
befoul themselves in the thick dust! With how much blood will
the red earth be stained! Neither your god-like sword nor your
right hand, Mezentius,[71] nor the savage force of your spirit will
save you from a violent death, but you will join your son in death
and in the tomb. But where are you rushing heedlessly, warrior   290
maid,[72] through your excessive love of plunder and glory? Why do
you not see the cruel ambush and the spear that will strike you

inconsulta, ruis? Quin saevas, bellica virgo,
insidias prius et venientem respicis hastam?
Tuque, miser, pone o rapti mala gaudia baltei
295   et caesi exuvias pueri invidiamque deorum,
Turne, cave; dabis, heu, poenas, dabis, improbe, et istam
Evandro debes animam atque ultricibus umbris.
Sic tandem Iliacas properans pensare ruinas
ad Teucros fessis revolat Victoria pinnis.
300   Grande tamen vobis leti solamen honesti,
magnanimi heroes nati felicibus astris,
afferet Aonius iuvenis, cui dia canenti
facta virum totis pariter praeconia linguis
solvet Fama loquax, cui dulci semper ab ore
305   roscida mella fluent cuiusque Acheloia Siren
gestiet innocuo divina poemata cantu
flectere, cui blandis insidet Suada labellis,
cui decus omne suum cedet stupefacta vetustas.
Ipsa illi, quem vix ducibus largiris, honorem
310   sponte feres totoque assurges, Roma, theatro.'
    Haec ubi veridico fudit de pectore Manto,
composuit vultum teneroque arrisit alumno;
osculaque ore legens sacrum inspiravit amorem
afflavitque animum tenuesque recessit in auras.
315   Plauserunt hilares ad tanta oracula Musae,
plauserunt nymphae, quique alto e vertice montis
adfuerat, capripes concussit cornua faunus
et triplices carmen scripsere adamante sorores.
    Vos age nunc alacres certatim, Etrusca iuventus
320   Aoniis operata sacris, accurrite mecum
daedala perpetui visum monumenta poetae,
qualia nec castae peplis intexta Minervae
sollemni, veteres, lustro explicuistis, Athenae,
picta rubro quoties animantur proelia cocco,

down? And you, victim of fate, put aside the malignant joy you
derive from the plundered baldric and the spoils of the slain
youth,[73] beware the envy of the gods, Turnus; you will pay the   295
penalty, alas! You will pay dearly, miserable man, and you owe
your soul to Evander[74] and the avenging shades. So at last, hasten-
ing to make amends for the fall of Troy, Victory flies back to the
Trojans on tired wings.

And yet, great-souled heroes born under favorable stars, an   300
Aonian youth will bring great consolation to you for your honor-
able death. Eloquent Fame, from whose sweet mouth dewy honey
shall always flow, shall bestow praises on him with all her tongues
for his celebrating the divine feats of heroes; a Siren, daughter of
Acheloüs, will eagerly desire to sing his divine poems in an un-   305
harmful song; the goddess Persuasion will sit upon his charming
lips; antiquity, in wonder, will cede all its glory to him. Rome, you
will spontaneously render him the honor which you reluctantly as-
sign to great warriors, and you will rise to your feet, with the
whole theater, to acclaim him."[75]   310

When Manto had uttered these words from her prophetic
breast, she composed her facial expression and smiled at her young
charge; and kissing him she breathed sacred love into him and in-
fused her spirit into him, and then vanished into the air. The
Muses jubilantly expressed their approval at these portents, as did   315
the nymphs; and from a far-off mountaintop a goat-footed fawn
shook its horns, and the three sisters wrote down their oracle in
adamantine letters.

Come, then, Tuscan youths, having performed the sacred rites
of the Muses, accompany me, rivalling each other in enthusiasm to   320
see the Daedalian monuments of the eternal poet. Such monu-
ments you, Athens of old, did not succeed in embroidering on the
peplum of chaste Minerva[76] on the occasion of the quinquennial
celebrations, when the battles painted in scarlet red came to life,
nor are they rivalled by the Seven Wonders spread over the im-

325   nec vetus immensum fuerint quae sparsa per orbem
       gloria septena celebrat spectacula fama.
       Nam neque belligeris Babylon pulsata quadrigis
       moenia nec liquido pomaria pendula caelo
       conferat, aut dextris constructa altaria Delos
330   cornibus, aut vasti molem Rhodes aurea Phoebi;
       non Cares, Mausole, tui caelamina busti,
       Phidiacum non Elis ebur, non ipsa superbas
       pyramidas iactet lascivi lingua Canobi.
       Namque haec aut valido Neptuni quassa tridenti
335   aut telo, Summane, tuo traxere ruinam,
       aut trucibus nimbis aut irae obnoxia Cauri,
       aut tacitis lenti perierunt dentibus aevi.
       At manet aeternum et seros excurrit in annos
       vatis opus: dumque in tacito vaga sidera mundo
340   fulgebunt, dum sol nigris orietur ab Indis,
       praevia luciferis aderit dum curribus Eos,
       dum ver tristis hiems, autumnum proferet aestas,
       dumque fluet spirans refluetque reciproca Tethys,
       dum mixta alternas capient elementa figuras,
345   semper erit magni decus immortale Maronis,
       semper inexhaustis ibunt haec flumina venis,
       semper ab his docti ducentur fontibus haustus,
       semper odoratos fundent haec gramina flores,
       unde piae libetis apes, unde inclyta nectat
350   serta comis triplici iuvenilis Gratia dextra.
         Et quis, io, iuvenes, tanti miracula lustrans
       eloquii, non se immensos terraeque marisque
       prospectare putet tractus? Hic ubere largo
       luxuriant segetes, hic mollia gramina tondet
355   armentum, hic lentis amicitur vitibus ulmus;
       illinc muscoso tollunt se robora trunco,
       hinc maria ampla patent, bibulis hoc squalet harenis

mense world, celebrated by ancient tradition. For Babylon cannot   325
compare with them the walls upon which war chariots coursed,
nor the gardens[77] hanging in the limpid air, nor can Delos com-
pare its altar made of horn,[78] nor can Rhodes the Golden[79] com-
pare its colossal statue of Apollo, nor the Carians the relief-work   330
of your sepulchre, Mausolus,[80] nor Elis the ivory statue[81] carved by
Phidias, nor can the tongue of lascivious Canopus[82] boast of the
proud pyramids. For these marvels were either destroyed by the
powerful trident of Neptune or fell victim to your thunderbolt,
Summanus,[83] or perished from exposure to violent storms or the   335
wrath of Caurus[84] or the silent tooth of remorseless time. But the
work of the poet remains forever and lasts through length of years.
As long as the wandering stars shall shine in the silent firmament,
as long as the sun shall rise from darkest India, as long as Aurora   340
shall precede the day in her light-bringing chariots, as long as sul-
len winter shall announce spring and summer autumn, as long as
seething Tethys[85] shall alternately ebb and flow, as long as the ele-
ments shall join together to take new form, the immortal glory of
great Maro will live on forever; these rivers will always flow in in-   345
exhaustible streams, learned draughts will always be drunk from
these fonts, these plants will always produce fragrant flowers, from
which, sacred bees, may you sip, and with them the youthful
Graces will plait splendid garlands in their hair.   350

And who, O my young men, contemplating the wonders of
such great eloquence, would not think that he is surveying the im-
mense expanses of land and sea? Here crops flourish in great
abundance; here the flock browses on tender grasses; here the elm
is adorned with the flexible vines; there the oaks rise up with their   355
mossy trunks; here vast seas unfold; this shoreline lies barren with
thirsty sands; from these mountains frozen streams flow down;

litus, ab his gelidi decurrunt montibus amnes;
huc vastae incumbunt rupes, hinc scrupea pandunt
360   antra sinus, illinc valles cubuere reductae
et discors pulchram facies ita temperat orbem.
Sic varios sese in vultus facundia dives
induit; et vasto nunc torrens impete fertur
fluminis in morem, sicco nunc aret in alveo.
365   Nunc sese laxat, nunc exspatiata coercet;
nunc inculta decet, nunc blandis plena renidet
floribus, interdum pulchre simul omnia miscet.
O vatum pretiosa quies! O gaudia solis
nota piis, dulcis furor, incorrupta voluptas
370   ambrosiaeque deum mensae! Quis, talia cernens,
regibus invideat? Mollem sibi prorsus habeto
vestem aurum gemmas, tantum hinc procul esto malignum
vulgus. Ad haec nulli perrumpant sacra profani.

here huge rocks loom up; here rocky caverns reveal their recesses; there secluded valleys open up; and thus the discordant aspect creates the beautiful harmony of the world. So rich eloquence assumes different appearances: now it is a torrent borne along by a powerful impetus like a river, now it lies parched in a dry river bed; now it releases itself; now after overflowing its bounds it hems itself in; now an unpolished style is fitting, now it is resplendent, filled with charming embellishments; and sometimes it combines them all beautifully together. O precious tranquillity of poets! O joys known only to the devout, sweet delirium, uncorrupted pleasure, and the ambrosial tables of the gods! Who, beholding such things, would be envious of kings? Let the malignant crowd have their finery, their gold, their jewels, as long as they stay at a distance. Let no profane persons invade these sacred precincts.

360

365

370

RUSTICUS

Angelus Politianus Iacobo Salviato suo S. D.

En Rusticum tibi. Id illi scilicet ab argumento inditum nomen. Tuo coactu prodit in vulgum; tibi est uni quidquid acciderit imputaturus. Iamne sentis quam tibi tuendus sit, vel tuo ipsius nomine vel meo? Tua enim fides in eo, meus honos agitur; cuius quidem etsi semper cura apud te iam inde a pueritia excubuit, tamen eum tueri nunc vel ob id ipsum impensius debes, quod es nuper Laurentio Medici principi viro, cuius ego cliens alumnusque sum, unus ex omni Florentina iuventute gener ascitus. Profer igitur in tali patrocinio auctoritatem omnem atque gratiam, quam videlicet tibi et viri excellentis affinitas et tua egregia indoles morumque suavitas conciliant. Vale, meque, ut facis, ama.

THE COUNTRYMAN

Angelo Poliziano to His Friend Jacopo Salviati,[1] Greeting.

Here is your *Countryman*. Obviously this name was given to it from the subject matter. At your instigation it appears in public; whatever happens will be laid to your charge. Do you not feel by now how much you are responsible for it, whether for your reputation or mine? Your good faith is at stake in it and my honor. Although you have exercised vigilant care for my honor since childhood, nevertheless you must protect it all the more now, because not long ago you were chosen out of all Florentine youth to be the son-in-law of Lorenzo de' Medici, our illustrious prince, whose client and protégé I am. Exhibit, therefore, in such patronage all the authority and favor that accrue to you from your relationship with so eminent a personage, as well as from your own excellent character and natural charm. Farewell, and love me, as you do.

Angeli Politiani silva cui titulus Rusticus
in poetae Hesiodi Vergilique Georgicon
enarratione pronuntiata

Ruris opes saturi gnavoque agitanda colono
munera et omniferae sacrum telluris honorem
ludere septena gestit mea fistula canna.
Fistula Mantoae quam nuper margine ripae
5   ipse renidenti dum dat mihi Tityrus ore:
'Hac, puer, Ascraeum repete,' inquit, 'harundine carmen.'
Pan, ades, et curvi mecum sub fornice saxi
versibus indulge, medio dum Phoebus in axe est,
dum gemit erepta viduatus compare turtur,
10   dum sua torquati recinunt dictata palumbes.
Hic resonat blando tibi pinus amata susurro,
hic vaga coniferis insibilat aura cupressis,
hic scatebris salit et bullantibus incita venis
pura coloratos interstrepit unda lapillos;
15   hic tua vicinis ludit lasciva sub umbris,
iamdudum nostri captatrix carminis, Echo.
     Felix ille animi divisque simillimus ipsis,
quem non mendaci resplendens gloria fuco
sollicitat, non fastosi mala gaudia luxus,
20   sed tacitos sinit ire dies et paupere cultu
exigit innocuae tranquilla silentia vitae,
urbe procul, voti exiguus; sortemque benignus
ipse suam fovet ac modico contentus acervo
non spes corde avidas, non curam pascit inanem;
25   securus quo sceptra cadant, cui dira minentur
astra et sanguinei iubar exitiale cometae.
Non illum fragilis favor indocilisque potenti

*A Silva of Angelo Poliziano Entitled The Countryman
Recited as an Introduction to Lectures
on the Poet Hesiod and the Georgics of Vergil*

The riches of the fertile farmlands, the labors that occupy the dili-
gent tiller of the soil, the sacred honor of the earth that produces
all things, these my seven-reeded pipe craves to sing, the pipe
which Tityrus[2] gave me recently with smiling countenance on the
banks of the Mantuan river, saying: "With this reed renew the   5
Ascrean song."[3] Pan, be with me, and under the vault of the
curved rock look favorably upon my verses, while Phoebus is mid-
way through the sky, while the turtledove, bereft of its companion,
moans, while the ringdoves repeat their sound. Here your beloved   10
pine makes its sweet whispering sound; here the restless breeze
whistles among the coniferous cypresses; here the limpid water
gushes forth, rushing headlong in bubbling currents, splashing
noisily over the colored pebbles; here your beloved Echo, who for
some time already has captured my song, sports playfully among
the nearby shadows.   15

Happy in spirit and comparable to the gods themselves is the
man who is not attracted by the lure of glory with its false splen-
dors or by the evil pleasures of haughty luxury, but allows the days
to go by quietly and in his modest way of life spends his days in   20
the silent tranquility of a blameless life, far from the city, with few
desires. He accepts his lot resignedly and is happy with his modest
possessions; he does not nurture avid hopes or empty cares in his
heart; he is unconcerned with the fall of kingdoms or with those
who are threatened by dreadful signs in the skies and the fatal   25
glare of a blood-red comet. Not carried away by the uncertain
breezes of popular favor, he will not be placed upon a throne, des-
tined to fall, by the common herd, who have not learned to keep

plebs servare fidem, evectum popularibus auris,
casuro imponit solio, nec ducit hiantem
30 huc illuc vanos ostentans purpura fasces.
Non mentem pavet ipse suam nec conscius omnes
exhorret strepitus nec edaci pectora culpa
carpitur occulte; non opportunus iniqui
iudicio vulgi aut celsa conspectus in arce
35 degeneri patet invidiae; non ipse vicissim
obliquo livore macet fetusque veneno
aestuat atque aliena oculis bona limat acutis.
Rure agit in vacuo spatiisque indulget aperti
aetheris, aut operi insudans aut ille supinos
40 evadens cursu in montes; hinc scilicet omnes
gratae epulae; nudis Acheloum in pocula palmis
advocat excussaeque cibos dant bracchia silvae
et fessa in duro renovantur membra cubili.
Maior quippe venit comitata labore voluptas,
45 nec satias dominam aut fastidia lenta sequuntur.
Ergo neque imbrifero pallens Autumnus hiatu,
nec malus hunc afflat rabioso Sirius astro,
saevave Rhiphaeae labefactant frigora brumae;
quippe hiemem excipere et ventos caelique ruinam
50 suetum atque octipedem nec opaco vertice Cancrum,
et Iove sub gelido nocturnos carpere somnos,
et pede concretas nudo calcare pruinas,
et perferre sitim et ieiunia solvere glande,
et lassare feras cursu et superare natatu
55 torrentem, et volucri fossam tramittere saltu,
et quercum annosam ferro obturbare bipenni.
Tum praedam extorquere lupo fascique maligno
subiecisse humeros et iniqui pondera rastri
praedura tractare manu et domitore lacerto
60 sub iuga cornigeri colla obluctantia tauri

faith with the powerful, nor does he allow himself to be dragged
hither and yon, his mouth agape, by the purple garb which prom-
ises empty symbols of power. He is not frightened at his own   30
thoughts, nor does his guilty conscience make him terrified at ev-
ery sound, nor does gnawing guilt eat secretly away at his heart.
He is not subject to the judgment of the prejudiced crowd nor is
he, descried in his lofty citadel, exposed to ignoble jealousy. He in   35
turn is not consumed by malicious envy nor does he seethe, swol-
len with envy's venom, nor does he detract from another's bless-
ings with sharp-eyed looks. He lives in the open countryside and
enjoys the wide vistas under an open sky, whether he be perspiring
at his work or escaping into the sloping hillside. From here come   40
all his delicious repasts: he fetches water from the springs in the
palms of his hands and with the strength of his arms he shakes
down his sustenance from the trees, and his tired limbs are revived
on the hard couch. For Pleasure is greater when it is accompanied
by labor and you do not sate her as your mistress nor does linger-
ing ennui follow. Therefore, neither pale autumn with its rain-   45
bringing maw nor malignant Sirius with its raging constellation
bring blight upon him, nor does the rigid cold of winter coming
down from the Riphaean range[4] make him quiver, since he is ac-
customed with head uncovered to resist the wintry winds and the
fury of the heavens and eight-footed Cancer, and to catch his   50
nightly sleep under a freezing sky, and to tread barefooted upon
the frosty ground, and to endure thirst and satisfy his hunger with
acorns, and to tire wild animals in the chase, and swim across the
torrent, and traverse the ditches with a nimble leap, and topple the   55
ancient oak with his two-edged axe. And then, in addition, he can
rob the wolf of its prey, shoulder a cumbrous bundle of faggots,
drag the weight of the cruel mattock in his rough hands, and with
overpowering strength submit to the yoke the rebellious neck of
the horned bull and engage infuriated bears at close quarters.   60

ducere et iratis concurrere cominus ursis.

    Hinc agilis subit ora vigor robustaque magno
pectore vis habitat fortesque animosa tuentur
membra tori et crudo tendunt se robore nervi;

65   hinc facies procera, hinc fronti Martius horror.
Quod si bella vocent, quis ad aspera promptior arma?
aut quis equum sternacem artis fregisse lupatis
acrior, aut fortem mucrone haurire cruorem,
aut torquere sudem, aut nervo exturbare sagittam,

70   aut praepilatis aciem perrumpere contis?
Quis certet duro agricolae? seu ducere vallum,
seu sit opus celso praecingier aggere castra,
seu fronte adversa tormentum figere aenum,
quod tonitru horrifico magnas sternentia turres

75   ardua fulmineo iaculetur saxa rotatu;
seu vigil insomnem peragat custodia noctem,
seu tacitum rapiatur iter, seu parcere parto
conveniat, si fors lenta obsidione premantur.
Scilicet his Babylon dextris Nabataeaque regna

80   creverunt; hic Mopsopio delectus ab arvo
miles Achaemenium Marathonis in aequore Persen
contudit; his adiuta viris, se Romula tellus
imposuit mundo et rerum tractavit habenas.

    Nunc age, quae studia agricolis industria sollers

85   extudit atque operum quanta experientia dicam.
Protinus extremo cum iam Boreas autumno
incubuit terris, primo cum frigore tactae
labuntur frondes maternaque bracchia linquunt,
nec cariem caesae formidant robora silvae,

90   ecce sagax tacitam venientis rusticus anni
curam corde coquit, qua bubus ab arbore plaustrum
dedolet, unde iuga et curvum fabricetur aratrum.
Nec mora, quin veteris truncata cacumina fagi

For this reason a lively energy shines forth in their faces and ro-
bust strength resides in their broad chests, and powerful muscles
protect their spirited limbs, and their sinews are stretched taut in
youthful strength. Hence their tall stature, the warlike grimness in
their face. And if war calls, who is more ready for fierce battle? Or   65
who is more keen to tame the rearing horse with the tight jagged-
toothed bit? Or to drain the blood of the brave foe with his
sword? Or to hurl the spear? Or let fly the arrow from his bow?
Or break through the front lines armed with bent lance? Who can   70
rival the sturdy farmer, whether it be necessary to build a palisade
or surround the camp with a high rampart, or to set in front of the
enemy a bronze catapult, which with terrifying thunder launches
huge boulders, lobbing them into the air, spinning swiftly, levelling
the large siege-towers; or to pass a sleepless night keeping watch or   75
complete a secret mission; or whether there be need to ration pro-
visions if they are confined by a long siege. Surely it was with such
manpower that Babylon and the kingdoms of Nabataea[5] grew; this
kind of soldier, recruited from the fields of Mopsopsia,[6] crushed   80
the Persian Achaemenid[7] on the plain of Marathon; with the help
of such men the land of Romulus imposed itself upon the world
and held the reins of power.

And now I shall tell what skills resourceful industry devised for
farmers and what experience they acquired in their labors. As   85
soon as Boreas has launched his attack upon the earth at the end
of autumn, when the leaves, touched by the cold, fall, leaving their
mother's arms, and the hard-woods that have been cut down in
the woods are in no fear of rotting, behold, the wise farmer broods
silently in his heart about the coming year, asking himself from   90
what tree he will hollow out a wagon for his oxen and build his
yokes and the curved plough. Without delay the trimmed tops of
the old beech and Chaonian oaks[8] fall, and the elm, stripped of its

Chaoniaeque cadant quercus nudataque ramos
95   ulmus et audaci laurus sonet icta securi;
quarum quaeque novam, fumo explorata calenti,
vertitur in faciem diversaque munia tractant.
Continuo auditus gruis inter nubila clangor
agricolam citat et crista spectabilis alta
100   auroram gallus vocat applaudentibus alis.
Excitat ille operum socios; simul horrida cautus
terga rudi centone fovet capitique galerum
induitur crudusque operit vestigia pero.
Hinc saturos iungens loris ad aratra iuvencos
105   increpitat stimulo; et cantu minuente laborem,
praelongis ferrata terit dentalia sulcis
ac late elicibus collectos exprimit imbres
ieiunamque fimo tellurem et rudere pascit.
Tum plenum farris laeva servante canistrum,
110   semina dispensat parca cerealia dextra;
quae ne iacta avidae populentur grana volucres
et praedam sublime ferant, it pone minutus
sarcula parva tenens puer et frugem obruit arvo.
At cum se Eois iam vespertinus ab undis
115   extulit Arcturus, cum versicoloribus ardet
terra comis rutilosque interviret herba colores,
Daulias et Getici tandem secura mariti
ales adest plausuque larem cantuque salutat,
rursum invadit opus; stivaeque innisus adunco
120   pone nigrescentes proscindit dente novales
quas rapidi soles urant gelidaeque pruinae.
Mox ubi iam sapiens coepit frondescere morus
(ante quidem sapiens, nunc ambitiosa), nec ullum
quae pariat pomum, sed serica pensa ministret,
125   ille aliam atque aliam culturam dulcis agelli
pertentans, truncos plantariaque infodit arvo;

branches, and the laurel resound with the blows of the bold axe; and each of them, seasoned by the hot smoke, assumes a new appearance and serves for different tasks. Immediately thereafter the clamor of the crane heard among the clouds rouses the farmer, and the cock, conspicuous with its tall crest, calls forth the dawn, clapping its wings. The farmer awakens his fellow workers; at the same time he prudently keeps his hairy back warm with a crude quilted cloak and puts on his skin cap and covers his feet with rough rawhide boots. Then, yoking the well-fed young bulls to the plough with straps, he rouses them with the goad; and lightening his labor with song, he wears down the iron share-beams in the long furrows and spreads the rain water that has collected in the furrow-drain and nurtures the hungry land with manure and marl. Then, holding a basket of wheat in his left hand, he scatters the seeds sparingly with his right hand; and so that the greedy birds will not ravage the planted seed and carry off their plunder into the air, a young boy holding a small hoe walks behind him and covers the seed with earth. But when, as evening draws nigh, Arcturus[9] has risen from the Eastern waves, and the earth glows with its vari-colored leaves, and the golden red colors blend in with the green grass, and when the bird of Daulis,[10] finally liberated from her Getic spouse, appears and greets her home with song and a beating of her wings, the farmer enters again upon his labors. Leaning on the shaft of the plough-handle, he cleaves the fallow fields with the curved ploughshare, which turn black as he passes, so that the scorching sun and icy hoarfrost will penetrate it. Soon, when the wise mulberry tree begins to put forth its foliage (previously it was wise, now it is ambitious), since it does not bear any fruit, but quantities of silk to be spun, he makes trial of various cultivations in his cherished little plot of land, planting trees and cuttings in the soil; he does not neglect to entrust sinis-

nec pictas lugubre fabas, nec pabula parcit
vervacto mandare putri, glebasque bicorni
persequitur ferro et secat insuperabile gramen,
130   et montem caedit scrobibus fortique bidente
terga soli frangit; Bacchaeaque semina rectum
explicat in quincuncem et disserit ordine longo,
atque iterum atque iterum terra capita ima frequentat
et ramos tondet falce, atque impune fluentem
135   compescit vitem fingens et robore fulcit
deciduam caraeque haerentem in pectore matris
acclinat subolem sulco iuxtaque propagat,
aut ipso durus genetricis ab ubere flentis
abscissam rapit atque alio traducit alendam.
140   Quid dicam, externis cum se vernacula sucis
robora nobilitant peregrinaque segmine duri
accipiunt trunci aut discreto germina libro?
Namque oculis oculos non blandi tempora veris
iungere, sed mediis gaudet fervoribus aestas;
145   aestas congestos Cereris tritura maniplos,
aestas absconsum siliqua excussura legumen,
aestas qua grandes expectant horrea messes,
dum coacervatas eventilet area fruges.
Tum sola pulverei pinguescunt arida campi
150   solvunturque putres glebae ac peritura lupini
germina parturiunt; tum clivo rauca sonantes
eliciuntur aquae praecepsque recumbit agro fons.
Post ubi iam medio vestigia librat in axe
ensifer Orion croceoque insignis amictu
155   aspicit Arcturum pulsa Pallantias umbra,
sentibus horrentes aperit iam vinea saepes
aureolamque metit lentis de vitibus uvam
vinitor et fetos rubicundo nectare fructus,
quos coniunx, quos virgo comes, par vertice matri,

ter-colored beans and fodder to the crumbly, newly ploughed land, and he works the glebe with his two-pronged pitchfork and cuts the overgrown grass and intersects the slope with trenches and breaks the surface of the soil with his strong hoe and arranges the vines in the orderly quincunx pattern,[11] planting them in long rows, and again and again mounds up the soil at the base of the trees and prunes the branches with his pruning-hook, curbs the rampant growth, giving shape to the vine, and supports drooping vines with a prop. He places in the furrow the shoot that is attached to the bosom of its dear mother and propagates it nearby or cruelly tears it away from the breast of its weeping mother and transplants it elsewhere for its nurture.

What shall I say of the time when our native oaks are ennobled with the sap of other trees and receive alien buds through a cutting in their hard trunk or the graft is inserted into the bark. The sweet spring season is not the time for budding, but the intense heat of midsummer. It is summer that will thresh the stacked up sheaves of grain, summer that will shake out the hidden pulse from its pod, summer when the granaries await the abundant harvests, until the threshing floor will have winnowed the heaps of grain. Then the arid soil of the dusty fields grows rich, and the crumbling clods are loosened and the lupins produce their perishable sprouts; then the streams burst forth from the slopes with raucous sound and the water descends precipitously upon the fields, inundating them. Afterwards when sword-bearing Orion steadies his steps midway across the sky, and clad in her saffron mantle, the daughter of the Titan Pallas[12] catches sight of Arcturus when the shades of night have fled away, the vineyard opens up its hedges bristling with thorns, and the vine-grower picks the golden bunches of grapes from the pliant vines and their fruit rich with ruby-colored nectar, which his wife and his young daughter, equal to her mother in height, carry away in hampers or in smooth

160 aut cista exportant aut rasilibus calathiscis;
nec sentitur onus studio, levat ipsa laborem
sedulitas: quin frugiferos curvantia ramos
poma sinu baccasque ferunt ficumque nucemque.
Nec nihil addit hiems: nigros tum laurea fetus
165 exuitur, tum myrta legunt glandemque caducam
glaucaque Palladiae destringunt bracchia silvae.
Nocte autem ad lychnos aut iunco texit acuto
fiscellam, aut crates virgis aut vimine qualos
rusticus infinditque faces et robora valli,
170 dolia quassa novat ferramentisque repellit
scabritiem tritaque docet splendescere cote.
    Nam quid delicias memorem, quamque alta labori
otia succedant? Iam primum obsessa pruinis
cum iuga floriferi regelaverit aura Favoni,
175 suave serenato rident vaga sidera caelo,
suave ciet tardos per sudum luna iuvencos;
ipsa quoque aetherii melius nitet orbita fratris,
terque quaterque manu madidantes nectare crines
exprimit et glebas fecundis roribus implet
180 vecta Medusaeo Tithonia praepete coniunx.
Alma novum tellus vultu nitidissima germen
fundit et omnigenis ornat sua tempora gemmis:
Idalio pudibunda sinus rosa sanguine tinguit,
nigraque non uno viola est contenta colore,
185 albet enim, rubet et pallorem ducit amantum;
ut sunt orta cadunt, nive candidiora ligustra,
nec longum durant calathos imitata patentes
lilia, sed longum stant purpurei amaranthi.
Hic Salaminiaci scribunt sua nomina flores,
190 hic gratum Cereri plenumque sopore papaver
oscitat, hic inhiat sibimet Narcissus; at illic
Corycios alit aura crocos notumque theatris

wicker baskets. In their enthusiasm they do not sense the weight,   160
their eagerness lightens the task; indeed they carry in their aprons
the fruit that bends the fruitful branches, and berries and figs and
nuts. Winter also has its chores: it is then that the laurel loses its
dark berries, then that they pick the fruit of the myrtle and the
fallen acorns, and strip the branches of the gray-green tree of   165
Pallas Athena. At night by lamplight the farmer weaves small
wicker baskets with pointed rushes, or trellises with twigs, or osier
hampers, and he splits wood for torches and the posts for the en-
closures; he repairs the damaged earthenware vessels, and removes
the rust from the iron tools and makes them shine, rubbing them   170
with a whetstone.

And why should I relate his pleasures and the profound relax-
ation that follows upon his labors? As soon as the breezes of
flower-bearing Favonius[13] have thawed the high slopes, previously
covered with snow, the wandering stars smile sweetly in the serene
sky, the moon gently drives its slow-moving bullocks through the   175
clear bright sky, the disk of her celestial brother shines brighter
also, and the spouse of Tithonus,[14] borne by the winged Pegasus,
wrings out her locks, drenched with nectar, and bathes the earth
with fecund dew. Life-giving earth with radiant countenance pro-   180
duces new shoots and adorns her temples with buds of every kind:
the blushing rose tinges her breast with Idalian[15] blood; the dark
violet is not content with one color (for it is white, it is red, or
it takes on the pallid hue of lovers); as in their birth so do the   185
privets die, whiter than snow, nor do the lilies that look like wide-
mouthed goblets last long, but the scarlet amaranthus lasts a long
time; here the flowers of the hero from Salamis[16] write their name,
here the poppy dear to Ceres and full of sleep yawns; here Narcis-   190
sus is enraptured with himself; but here the breeze nurtures the
Corycian[17] saffrons, and with its breath disperses through the soft

aera per tenerum flatu dispergit odorem.
Nec iam flammeolae connivent lumina caltae
195 nec melilotos abest; Tyrium seges illa ruborem
induit, hic vivo caespes se iactat in auro;
hae niveos, hae cyaneos superare lapillos
contendunt herbae vernantque micantia late
gramina per tumulos perque umbriferas convalles
200 perque amnis taciti ripas; atque omnia rident,
omnia luxuriant et amica luce coruscant.
Parturiunt stipulae frugem et genitalibus auris
pervia turgescunt lactentibus hordea culmis;
palmes agit rupto lacrimantes cortice gemmas,
205 seque rudes primis monstrant in vitibus uvae.
Dulce virent tenerae modo nata cacumina silvae
succrescuntque piae pullorum examina matri;
ipsa sibi ignotas miratur adultera frondes
arbor et ascitis nativas inserit umbras.
210 Auricomae, iubare exorto, de nubibus adsunt
Horae, quae caeli portas atque atria servant,
quas Iove plena Themis nitido pulcherrima partu
edidit, Ireneque Diceque et mixta parenti
Eunomie, carpuntque recentes pollice fetus.
215 Quas inter, Stygio remeans Proserpina regno,
comptior ad matrem properat; comes alma sorori
it Venus et Venerem parvi comitantur Amores,
Floraque lascivo parat oscula grata marito;
in mediis, resoluta comas, nudata papillas,
220 ludit et alterno terram pede Gratia pulsat.
Uda choros agitat nais, decurrit oreas
monte suo, linquunt faciles iuga celsa napaeae
nec latitat sub fronde dryas; non iubila fauni
fundere, non iunctis satyri dare sibila cannis,
225 nec querulae cessant tenerum tinnire volucres;

air the perfume known to the theaters. The flaming marigolds no
longer close their eyes, nor is the melilot absent; there the field
clothes itself in Tyrian purple,[18] here the meadow vaunts itself in   195
living gold; some grasses seek to surpass pearls, others to surpass
emeralds; they bring their vernal splendor everywhere, over the
rounded hills and through the shaded glens and along the banks
of the silent river; and all things are smiling, all things flourishing,   200
and they emit a friendly light. The stalks produce the grain and
with the creative breezes the perforated ears of barley begin to
swell their stems full of juice; the vine-shoot breaks through its
sheath and puts forth buds exuding juices and the unripe bunches
of grapes appear on the early vines. The nascent treetops in the   205
young forest show fresh green growth, and swarms of shoots
spring up at the feet of their pious mother; the adulterous tree
marvels at the foliage unknown to it and joins his native shadows
to those newly acquired.

At first light of day the golden-haired Hours[19] who guard the   210
accesses and gates of heaven, descend from the clouds; lovely
Themis, impregnated by Jupiter, brought them forth in a splendid
birth: Irene, Dike and Eunomia,[20] who lay with her father, pick
the newly grown flowers; among them Proserpina,[21] more adorned
than her companions, returning from the Stygian realm, hastens   215
to her mother. Bounteous Venus accompanies her sister and the
little Cupids accompany Venus, and Flora[22] lavishes welcome
kisses on her lusty husband. Between them, her hair loosened, her
breasts bare, a Grace dances with alternating step; a dripping   220
naiad[23] leads the dance, an oread runs down from her mountain,
the indulgent Napaean maidens leave their elevated summits, and
the dryad no longer hides beneath the foliage; the fauns do not
cease to utter their joyous sounds, nor the satyrs to blow on their
Pan pipes nor the plaintive birds to make their soft, shrill sound.
The halcyon weeps in the midst of the waves, Philomela in the   225

45

fluctibus alcyone, densa philomela sub umbra,
canus olor ripis, tecto vaga plorat hirundo;
lene susurrat apis plenoque saporibus alveo
candida multiforae solidat fundamina cerae.
230 Colludunt per prata greges atque omne beato
flagrat amore nemus; iuvenem lasciva maritum
fert equa, fert tergo salientem bucula taurum,
saetigeraeque subant matres, decertat amator
fronte aries, avidos olidum pecus accipit hircos;
235 spectant innisi baculis gaudentque magistri.
Inde ubi praegnantes partu Lucina recenti
solvit, ut exaequet numero fetura parentes,
ipse rudem nec adhuc vestigia certa prementem
fert subolem gremio, sed ovem gracilemve capellam
240 enisas humero subit atque in stramine molli
componit sensim pastor stabuloque recondit.
Mox ut convaluere, rubos haec rupibus altis,
illa recens campo gramen decerpit aprico,
aut dulcis gelido delibant amne liquores,
245 ut sua conclusis ne desint pocula natis
utque fluat plenis dives mulsura papillis.
Subrumi expectant haedique agnique petulci,
cornigerasque vocant tremulo clamore parentes.
Bruta gregem plenum densis alit uberibus sus
250 exporrecta solo et grunnitu allectat amico
fellantis turpique luto se immunda volutat;
radices eadem calloso avidissima rostro
eruit et bulbum aut madida se pulte saginat.
Flet vitulum moesta absentem mugitibus altis
255 mater et immensam raucis miseranda querelis
silvam implet; boat omne nemus vallesque lacusque;
illa nigros late lucos saltusque peragrat
crebra gemens, crebra ad montem stabulumque revisit

dense shade, the white swan on the riverbank, the errant swallow
on the rooftop. The bee buzzes softly and in sweet-smelling hives
solidifies the white foundations of the many-celled wax. The herds
play together over the meadows and the whole woodland burns   230
with love; the frisky mare submits to her young mate, the heifer
lets the bull mount her from behind, the bristly female boars are
in heat, the lustful ram does battle with his horns and the foul-
smelling herd of she-goats welcomes the lustful males. Leaning on
their staffs, the herdsmen look on and enjoy the spectacle. Then   235
when Lucina[24] has delivered the pregnant mothers, which have
just given birth, so that the number of offspring equals that of par-
ents, the shepherd takes into his arms the new-born young whose
footing is still uncertain, but the frail sheep or goat that have just
given birth he carries on his shoulders and gently places in the soft
straw and in the shelter of the stable. When they have regained   240
their strength the goats crop the brambles on the high crags and
the sheep browse on the new grass in the sunny plains, or savor
the sweet waters of the icy stream, so that the newly-born in the
enclosure will not lack liquid nourishment and rich milk will flow   245
from their full udders. The butting, suckling kids and lambs await
them and call out to their horned mothers with tremulous voice.
The heavy sow nourishes its full litter with her thick-set udders,
stretched out on the ground, and with an affectionate grunt en-
courages the suckling piglets, and covered with slime, rolls around   250
in the filthy mud; with her rough snout she greedily digs up roots
and bulbs or stuffs herself with crushed spelt soaked in water.

With loud lowing the mournful mother weeps over her lost
calf[25] and pitifully fills the immense woodland with her piercing   255
cries; the whole wood reverberates, the valleys and the lakes; she
wanders far and wide through dark groves and thickets, moaning
unceasingly and frequently returning to the mountain and the sta-

tabescens desiderio; non ulla dolorem
260   pabula nec salicum frondes nec gramina rore
sparsa levant, non quae viridi vaga flumina ripa
perspicuam tenui deducunt murmure lympham.
Prata tener persultat equus libatque volucri
aequora summa fuga aut alti subit aspera montis
265   in iuga saxosumque amnem pede plaudit inermi.
Cui pulchro micat acre caput luduntque decorae
fronte comae, vibrant aures, atque orbe nigranti
praegrandes exstant oculi; tum spiritus amplis
naribus it fervens, stat cervix ardua, qualem
270   praefert Marmaricis metuenda leonibus ales,
ales quae vigili lucem vocat ore morantem.
Crescunt spissa toris lateque animosa patescunt
pectora consurguntque humeri et iam sessile tergum est,
spinaque depressos gemino subit ordine lumbos
275   et castigatum cohibent crassa ilia ventrem;
fundunt se laetae clunes subcrispaque densis
cauda riget saetis et luxuriantia crebrae
velant colla iubae ac dextra cervice vagantur.
Tum tereti substricta genu mollissima flectit
280   crura ferox, celsum ingrediens fremituque superbit;
grande sonat tornata cavo brevis ungula cornu,
ingenti referens Corybantia cymbala pulsu.
    O dulces pastoris opes! O quanta beatum
quam tenet hunc tranquilla quies! Ut pectore toto
285   laetitiam totaque fovet bona gaudia mente!
Nempe odii fraudumque expers, exemptus inani
ambitione vacansque metu, spe liber et insons,
nativo cultu et gaza praedives agresti,
ipse sibi vivit nullo sub teste suoque
290   pendet ab arbitrio, suus ipse est censor et alto
calcat opes animo ac regum deridet honores.

ble, wasting away with longing. No fodder nor willow leaves nor grass sprinkled with dew can soothe her sorrow, nor the wander- 260
ing streams that carry the clear waters along their green banks with sweetly murmuring sound. The young stallion leaps over the meadows and skims over the surface of the plains in swift flight or scales the rugged ridges of a high mountain and dashes into the pebbled stream with unshod foot. The splendid animal's fierce 265
head flickers, his elegant mane plays upon his forehead, his ears quiver, and his huge eyes stand out in their black sockets; then a fiery breath issues from his large nostrils; he holds his neck high like the crest of the bird feared by Libyan lions, the bird that calls 270
with its vigilant cry the slowly approaching day. His vigorous chest grows strong with thickset muscles and opens out broadly; his shoulders develop; his back is ready for a rider; a double ridge runs along his loins and his stout flanks support his firm stomach. His 275
sleek haunches broaden out, and his slightly wavy tail is stiff with dense bristles, and his thick mane veils his sturdy neck and flutters over his right shoulder; then, drawing in his rounded knee, he bends his supple legs high-spiritedly, and rearing up as he ad-
vances, he neighs proudly; the concave horn of his short, rounded 280
hoof creates a loud sound, recalling Corybantic[26] cymbals as it beats the ground.

O, the shepherd's sweet riches! What tranquil peace preserves his happiness! How it maintains gladness in his heart and nur-
tures honest joys in his spirit! Free of hatred and deceit, innocent 285
of empty ambition and immune from fear, untrammeled in his hopes and guiltless, by his ancestral way of life and the riches of the fields a very rich man, he lives for himself with no one to ob-
serve him; a free agent, he is his own critic, and haughtily tramples 290
on great possessions and derides the honors of kings. He does not have oak timbers supported by columns of Taenarian marble,[27]

Si non Taenareis illi stant fulta columnis
robora caelatumque alte laquearia subter
ridet ebur postemve silex asaroticus ornat;
295　　nec Maurusiacos pulchrae testudinis orbis
Delphica sustentat, nec docto trita Myroni
pocula multiplici florent radiantia gemma,
aut bis in Herculea Milesia vellera concha
versantur tenuique satur lanugine bombyx
300　　luteolos follis pretiosaque fila relinquit;
textile nec tenero subtegmine fulgurat aurum
spirantes referens vultus, quae Pergamos olim
artifici descripsit acu, quae stamina Memphis,
quae Tyros et Babylon radio pinxere sonanti.
305　　　　At iacet in molli proiectus caespite membra,
qua cavus exesum pumex testudinat antrum,
quave susurranti crinem dat aquatica vento
arbor, et aut calamos aut fixa hastilia iungit
cortice statque levi casa frondea nisa tigillo,
310　　quam metuant intrare pavor curaeque sequaces,
sub qua iucundos tranquillo pectore sensus
nutrit inabruptoque fovet sua corpora somno
silvarum et pecoris dominus ; stant sedula circum
turba canes audaxque Lacon acerque Molossus.
315　　Dant ignem extritum silices, dant flumina nectar
hausta manu, dat ager Cererem; non caseus aut lac
lucorumve dapes absunt; stat rupibus ilex,
mella ferens trunco plenoque cacumine glandem.
Illi sunt animo rupes frondosaque tesqua,
320　　et specus et gelidi fontes et roscida tempe,
vallesque Zephyrique et carmina densa volucrum,
et nymphae et fauni et capripedes satyrisci,
Panque rubens et fronte cupressifera Silvanus,
Silenique senes subdivalesque Ithyphalli,

ivory carvings decorating the panelled ceilings, or a door-post
adorned with mosaics to give him pleasure; nor does he possess a
tripod table with a top made of Mauretanian[28] citrus-wood and
decorated with tortoise-shell overlay; his goblets were not polished   295
by a masterful Myron[29] and do not gleam with innumerable gems;
he has no Milesian wool[30] dipped twice in Herculean purple,[31] and
the silk-worm, rich in its soft downy substance, does not deposit
its yellow cocoons and precious thread for him; and in his humble   300
abode there is no glitter of gold woven into the delicate fabric de-
picting life-like features, or the finery that Pergamum[32] once de-
signed with skillful needlework, or that Memphis,[33] Tyre and Bab-
ylon depicted with the noisy shuttle.

   But he lies on the soft turf with his limbs stretched out, where   305
the hollow pumice rock forms the vault of an eroded cave, where
the aquatic willow yields its tresses to the whispering wind. And
he joins together reeds or firm stakes with bark, and his leafy hut
takes shape, resting on a flimsy plank, where anxiety and persis-
tent cares fear to enter, where he nurtures happy feelings in his   310
peaceful heart and relaxes his body in uninterrupted sleep, master
of the woods and of his flock; his watchful pack of dogs stand
round him, the intrepid Laconian[34] and the fierce Molossian[35]
hound. The flint-stones rubbed together produce fire, the rivers
supply him with nectar that he scoops up with his hands, the field   315
yields grain; neither cheese nor milk nor fruits of the forest are
lacking; on the high rocks the holm-oak stands, yielding honey
from its trunk and acorns in abundance from its peak. He has at
heart the rocks and the leafy wilds and the cave and the icy
streams, dewy valleys and glens, and zephyrs and unending songs   320
of birds, and nymphs and fawns and goat-footed satyrs, and ruddy
Pan and Silvanus[36], his brow garlanded with cypress, and the old
Sileni[37] and the Priapuses[38] that live in the open air, and Pales[39]
dwelling in the mountains, and the god who gladdened the pasture

325 et montana Pales et quo pastore Pherei
 gaudebant campi et crinem resoluta Mimallon,
 et qui cornigera bicolores fronte corymbos
 pampineamque manu tenera quatit Evius hastam.
 Semper amor, semper cantus et fistula cordi est,
330 semper odorati Veneris stipendia flores
 vitarumque altrix urbi male nota voluptas;
 talibus in studiis pastor molle exigit aevum.

  Post ubi raucisonae pinna vibrante cicadae
 increpuere ardensque metentibus ingruit aestus,
335 paulisper tum cessat opus saxique sub umbra
 prostrati indulgent genio. Non mollia pleno
 desunt vina cado, non lacti mixta polenta,
 aut pinguis tergum vitulae placidusque sonorae
 lapsus aquae crinemque aurae frontemque lacessunt.
340 Inde opus integrant, donec sub nocte coruscent
 flammigero parvae stellantes clune volucres.
 Ecce autem dulces labris pater ingerit uvas
 Autumnus crebraeque elisus verbere plantae
 it per praela latex puerique examine denso
345 exsultant lasciva cohors circumque supraque.
 Ille manu panda pronus bibit, alter ab ipso
 sugit musta lacu crepitantibus hausta labellis,
 hic sua suspensum resupinus in ora racemum
 exprimit, hic socii patulos irrorat hiatus
350 irriguumque mero sordet mentumque sinusque
 ebriaque incertis titubant vestigia plantis.

  Postquam acris successit hiems et pendula tectis
 diriguit glacies, larga strue tollitur alte
 collucetque focus; coeunt vicinia simplex
355 una omnes, iuvenesque probi materque severa
 coniuge cum duro et pueris et virgine grandi,
 convigilantque hilares et primae tempora noctis

lands of Pherae,[40] and the Bacchante with her disheveled hair, and 325
Bacchus who shakes the two-colored clusters of ivy-berries on his
horned head and holds in his delicate hand the thyrsus covered
with vine-shoots. Always love, always song and the pipe he has in
his heart, always fragrant flowers, the tribute offered to Venus, and 330
pleasure, sustainer of life, a rare quality of the city.

Then when the loud cicadas have begun their din with their
whirring wings, and sultry summer has descended upon the har-
vesters, work stops for a while, and stretched out in the shade of a
rock they indulge themselves: sweet wine is not lacking in their 335
full jugs, nor polenta mixed with milk, nor the meat of a fat calf
and the placid flow of a gurgling brook, while the breezes caress
their hair and their brow. Afterwards they return to their work,
until at nightfall the tiny star-like fireflies emit flashes of light 340
from their fiery abdomens. Behold, father Autumn now brings
sweet grapes in his lips, and the juice, squeezed out by the re-
peated pounding of feet, flows through the wine-presses, and the
children swarm around the vats in playful groups. One, leaning 345
forward, drinks the new wine in his cupped hands, another sucks
it right out of the vat, quaffing it, making slurping sounds with his
lips; another, leaning back and holding a bunch of grapes over his
head, squeezes the juice on to his face while another pours it into
the wide-open mouth of his companion and soaks his chin and
chest with wine, and on unsteady feet they totter about, inebri- 350
ated.

When harsh winter has arrived and the ice hanging from the
roof has hardened, and the hearth, heaped up high, shines
brightly, the simple people of the neighborhood come together,
virtuous young men, a severe mother with her sturdy spouse, her 355
small children and grown daughter, and they stay up late, having a
good time and enjoying the first hours of the night, driving away

decerpunt, molli curas abigente Lyaeo.
Mutuaque inter se ludunt: tum tibia folle
360   lascivum sonat inflato, tum carmina cantant,
carmina certatim cantant; tum tenta recusso
tympana supplodunt baculo et cava cymbala pulsant,
et laeti saltant et tundunt aeribus aera,
et grave conspirat cornu tuba flexilis unco
365   conclamantque altum unanimes tolluntque cachinnos.
    Porro autem, quanta est differtae copia villae
quamque penu dives! Neque enim vel frugibus hornis
horrea sufficiunt vel odoro dolia musto,
testaque Palladiis iam non vacat ulla trapetis.
370   Terga suis pendent fumoso sordida tigno,
pertica pensilibus oneratur longa racemis;
non uvae arentes, non pruna et Carica desunt,
sorbaque cum cerasis duroque putamine clausa
Persica nux regumque altas imitata coronas
375   mespila, cumque piris miserorum munus amantum
iam laxum in rugas malum decoctaque aenis
defruta et omphacinus liquor et lacrimosa sinapis
et meditata novos Sicyonia bacca sapores.
Tum sapa melque recens edulcatique lupini
380   et prunae increpitans balanus contextaque cannis
fiscina lacte madens et durati sale fungi;
annonam facilem vicinus suggerit hortus.
Murmur apricantes nivea dant turre columbi,
expandunt alas et amicam blanda rogantes
385   oscula, circumeunt insertantque oribus ora;
iam vicibus nido incubitant genetrixque paterque,
iamque ova excudunt natisque implumibus escam
commansam alternant rostellaque hiantia complent.
    Adde gregem cortis cristatarumque volucrum
390   induperatores, laterum qui sidera pulsu

their cares with mellow wine. They joke with one another, then
filling their lungs, they play a lively tune on the reed-pipe; then
they sing songs, then vie with one another in song; then they beat   360
the tight-drawn drums with vibrating stick, and they strike the
hollow cymbals and dance gaily; bronze clashes on bronze, and the
versatile trumpet sounds deep tones together with the curved horn
and all shout aloud with one accord and raise peals of laughter.   365

On top of that, what abundance in the well-stocked farmhouse!
How rich in provisions! The granaries do not suffice for the sea-
son's crops or the huge earthenware receptacles for the fragrant
must, and there are no empty jars in Athena's mill.[41] The pig's
hindquarters hang from the blackened timbers; the long pole is   370
weighed down with hanging grapes; dried grapes and dried Carian
figs,[42] and plums are not lacking, nor sorbs and cherries, nor the
Persian nut closed in its hard shell, nor the medlar[43] that imitates
the exalted crown of kings, and there are apples, the gift of un-
happy lovers, already reduced to wrinkles, and pears and the grape   375
syrup boiled down in the bronze pots, the oil made from the un-
ripe grapes, and the mustard that brings tears to the eyes and the
Sicyonian olive[44] that produces new flavors. Then there is the
boiled-down must and this year's honey and sweetened lupins and
the chestnuts crackling on the glowing charcoal, and the pliant   380
baskets woven from rushes, oozing with milk, and the mushrooms
dried with salt. The nearby garden furnishes ready provisions.
The doves, basking in the sun, coo in their white-washed dove-
cote; they spread out their wings and, seeking sweet kisses, fly
around their mate and insert their beak in hers; soon father and   385
mother, taking turns, brood in the nest, and soon afterwards the
eggs break open and the parents take turns in bringing pre-masti-
cated food to the unfledged birds, filling their gaping little beaks.

Add to this the flock of the courtyard and the sovereigns of
crested fowl who drive the stars from the sky with a flap of their   390
wings and summon the Titan sun[45] with their wakeful song, and

explaudunt vigilique citant Titana canore
et regnum sibi Marte parant; quippe obvia rostris
rostra ferunt crebrisque acuunt assultibus iras;
ignescunt animis et calcem calce repulsant
395   infesto adversumque affligunt pectore pectus.
Victor ovans cantu palmam testatur et hosti
insultans victo, pavidum pede calcat iniquo.
Ille silet latebrasque petit dominumque superbum
ferre gemit; comes it merito plebs caetera regi,
400   formoso regi, cui vertice purpurat alto
fastigatus apex dulcique errore coruscae
splendescunt cervice iubae perque aurea colla
perque humeros it pulcher honos. Palea ampla decenter
albicat ex rutilo atque torosa in pectora pendet
405   barbarum in morem; stat adunca cuspide rostrum,
exiguum spatii rostrum, flagrantque tremendum
ravi oculi niveasque caput late explicat auris;
crura pilis hirsuta rigent iuncturaque nodo
vix distante sedet; durus vestigia mucro
410   armat, in immensum pinnaeque hirtique lacerti
protenti excurrunt duplicique horrentia vallo
falcatae ad caelum tolluntur acumina caudae.
Ipse salax totam fecundo semine gentem
implet et oblongo nunc terram scalpurit ungui
415   rimaturque cibos, nunc edita nubila visu
explorat cauto. Non illum squamea tuto
aggreditur serpens, non raptor ab aethere milvus.
Vocibus interea crebrum singultat acutis
parturiens coniunx, quae scilicet ova subinde
420   tollit anus signatque dies vigilemque lucernam
consulit, et lunae crescentis tempora servans,
ut primum gallina glocit, numero impare subdit;
versatisque diu sollers auscultat an intus

win their dominion by combat, for they battle beak against beak
and intensify their anger in repeated assaults; hearts aflame, they
repulse spur with hostile spur and knock against each other, breast
to breast. The victor in triumph proclaims his victory with a song,   395
jumps on the defeated foe, and tramples on the frightened adver-
sary with iniquitous foot. The other is silent; he seeks a place to
hide, he groans that he must submit to this proud master. The rest
of the crowd accompanies the deserving king, a fine-looking king
on whose uplifted head a crest glows with scarlet hue, and his   400
flashing neck-feathers fall pleasantly on the back of his neck in a
luminous sheen, and this beautiful adornment continues down his
golden neck and over his shoulders; the long wattles change in
color from red to white and hang down over his muscular chest
like a beard; he raises his beak with its hooked point, a beak of   405
miniature dimensions; his tawny eyes blaze menacingly; his head
spreads wide his snow-white ears; his feet bristle with shaggy
hairs, and the joint is not distant from the point of articulation; a
hard spur arms his feet; his feathers and shaggy wings spread out
immensely and the tips of his tail, sickle-shaped, shoot up towards   410
the sky like a double rampart. Highly sexed, he impregnates his
whole brood with fecund seed; at times he scratches the ground
with his oblong claw and searches for food; at other times with
cautious gaze he observes the clouds on high. The scaly snake does   415
not dare attack him nor the rapacious kite plummeting from the
sky. In the meantime his mate never ceases her cackling with pierc-
ing cries as she lays her eggs; the old farmwoman collects them
immediately and marks the day and examines it against the light
of the lantern. She observes the phases of the waxing moon, and   420
as soon as the hen clucks, she places the eggs under her in an un-
even number; and when the hen has sat on them for a long time,
she listens sharply to hear whether the unfledged chick is cheeping

pipiat involucer pullus tenerumque putamen
425 pertuderit molli rostro atque erumpere tentet.
　　Parte alia bifero plumosam corpore messem
nutrit et in crassa satur urinare lacuna
anser avet stagnumque super pede remigat udo
depictae cervicis anas, prolemque natatum
430 invitans, nunc exstat aquis, nunc mergitur alte.
Erigit explicitae gemmata volumina caudae
ambitiosus amans; at ficu et polline gliscit,
pellaci cantu deceptus ab aucupe turdus.
Insidit mutilo turtur seseque saginans
435 rauca gemit dulcesque miser suspirat amores.
Flet viduus perdix, queritur peregrina coturnix,
inclusi caveis. Hic caeca cuniculus antra
excavat, hic saepto praegnans lepus errat in amplo,
capreolique hinulique et aduncis dentibus apri;
440 hac stertunt glires, hac femina fetat echinus.
Daedala somniferos peragunt examina bombos
plenaque captivos servant vivaria pisces.
Scilicet his opibus placide sua corpora curant
dulciaque inter se laeti tellure magistra
445 officia exercent, ut quae neque ferre recuset
imperium neque non grandi mercede rependat,
si qua laborifero debentur farra colono.
　　Ille autem et volucri petit ardua sidera mente
scrutaturque sagax quae sit sententia divum:
450 quid quaeque emergens latitansve oriensve cadensve
stella paret; quid quadruplici celer afferat annus
cardine; quae sulcis, quae sint stata tempora messi;
quidque pecus vehat Olenium; qua grandine collis
trux Nepa dilapidet; quo turbine surgat Orion;
455 quos glomerent imbris aut pressus Arione delphin,
aut Pleas Arcturusque senex Hyadesque puellae;

and whether it has perforated the soft shell with its tender beak
and is trying to break out.   425

Elsewhere the goose looks after the downy harvest that its body
produces twice a year, and gorged with food, wants to dive into
the muddy ditch; the duck with its multi-colored neck rows its
way over the pond with its watery feet and, encouraging its young
to swim, skims over the surface of the water or dives down deeply. 430
The vain peacock rises up and unfolds the jeweled spirals of its
tail. But the thrush, deceived by the fowler's enticing call, is stuffed
with figs and flour. The turtledove is perched on a trunk and
stuffing itself full, moans mournfully and gloomily sighs over
sweet loves. The widowed partridge weeps, the migrant quail la-   435
ments, imprisoned in cages. Here a rabbit scoops out hidden
holes, here the prolific hare, kids, fawns and boars with their
curved tusks wander about in a spacious enclosure; there dormice
snore, here the female hedgehog gives birth. The skillful swarms   440
keep up their somniferous buzzing, and full fishponds hold the
captive fish. Obviously the farmers take good care of their bodies
with these riches and happily perform pleasant tasks among them-
selves, hearkening to the lessons of the earth, which does not re-
fuse to submit to their dominion and does not repay them with a   445
small reward if an amount of grain is owed the laborious farmer.

He also turns his alert mind to the stars above and wisely in-
quires into the meanings of the gods, what is the significance of
stars that appear or hide themselves from sight, that rise or fall;
what the swift-moving year brings in each season, what are the   450
fixed times for the furrows and for the harvest, what does the goat
of Olenus[46] bring, with what hailstorms will cruel Scorpion lash
the hills, in what storm will Orion arise; what rains will be accu-
mulated by the dolphin ridden by Arion,[47] or the Pleiades[48] or the 455
old man, Arcturus, or the maiden Hyades;[49] from where do the

unde bibant herbae divini pocula lactis;
cur rubigo satis uredoque vitibus obsit;
quid nebulas abigat tempestatesque repellat;
460   quod vento ingenium, quae nubes causa serenet;
quidque silens moneat quidque intermenstrua Phoebe,
vel cum plena meat, vel cum decrescere rursum
incipit. Ille etiam numeros legesque dierum
providus observat. Scit enim quid septima portet,
465   in qua nascentem excepit bona Delia fratrem;
scit quoque post decimam quid prima, quid altera luces
iniungant operum, quocirca aut vellera lanae
demetit aut gravido maturas mergite aristas
aut telam locat uxoris; nam pendula in ortu
470   posteriore suos etiam net aranea casses.
    Quae sequitur bona virgultis, inimica serendis
frugibus; ergo cavet quod obest quodque expedit urguet.
Novit enim quota connubiis, quota partubus obstet
aspiretve dies; quota pinguem emasculet haedum,
475   saeptaque circumdet pecori; quota iungat amantis
et clandestinos iubeat miscere susurros;
qua ponat canis hirritum malesuadaque pectus
cura nimis laceret; qua tristis oberret Erynnis
nocte magis. Secat ille suo sibi tempore lignum,
480   dolia degustat, subigit iuga ferre iuvencum.
De flabris quoque, de pluvia dulcique sereno
aut Lunae occasus aut idem consulit ortus:
tractat opus, si pura micet; sin atra recedat
aut quinto directa die aut medio orbe retusa,
485   nec gracili cornu aut triplici sit culta corona,
tecta subit metuens hiemis; si rubra coruscet,
tum vero expectat ventos, nec fallit eundem
quo Borean cornu, quo Cynthia provocet Austrum.
Consulit et Phoebi flammas: an grandinis augur